Praise for

GETTING TO GREAT

"A marvelous book! From the opening lines, I was hooked. It needs to be read by the masses, and the masses will be all the better for it. *Getting to Great* is a fast read with a deep message: We have the power to change our lives for the better—and Madelaine shows you how. Packed with wisdom, wit, and heartfelt honesty, *Getting to Great* reveals a practical roadmap to make the most of your time on this planet."

—Daniel L. Shapiro, PhD, Director, Harvard International Negotiation Program, and Author, *Negotiating the Nonnegotiable*

"Once I started, I couldn't put it down. An extraordinary examination of the journey and toolbox needed for *Getting to G.R.E.A.T.* Madelaine Weiss provides an engaging and very practical and realistic guidebook combining theory, philosophy, and practice for mapping one's successes in life!"

—Thomas W. Miller PhD, ABPP, Author of *Handbook of Stressful Transitions Across the Lifespan,* Professor Emeritus and Senior Research Scientist, Institute for Health, Intervention, and Policy, University of Connecticut

"*Getting to Great* is a wonderful, readable, usable, and thoughtful book with concrete strategies and examples for how to improve one's personal and work life, even when that effort seems daunting. This book should be celebrated for its honesty and deep understanding of how and why people feel, think, and act (or fail to act) in their personal and work lives. As an educator and specialist in trauma, I was especially impressed by her chapter on play. As she ably observes, we get stripped of our capacity to play at great cost to our well-being, and, for many reasons, play needs to be restored. In sum, the author's clear writing style and sense of humor make this a book both to read and re-read. I am on my second reading now."

—Karen Gross, Former College President, Senior Policy Advisor to the US Department of Education, Author of *Breakaway Learners* and *Trauma Doesn't Stop at the School Door*

"In *Getting to Great*, Madelaine Weiss formulates a 5-Step Strategy that brilliantly distills and eloquently illustrates—in straightforward terms—the combined wisdom of ancient philosophy and modern science for everyday life. I strongly recommend *Getting to Great* as a manual for work and life."

—**Steven Nisenbaum,** PhD, JD, Past President, Massachusetts Psychological Association, Ethico-legal Consultant at Harvard International Negotiation Program, Board of Directors Harvard Law School Association-MA

"A really enjoyable way to learn about ourselves. The tone made me feel I was having a personal conversation with the author. Easy to not only read but also to accept the challenges Madelaine Weiss puts in front of us. Men and women of all ages and stages in life can benefit from these insights on who we are and how we got here as well as what we can do moving forward. Especially helpful for those thinking of or needing career changes during this very difficult time. Wish I had had this when I was supervising teams. Can't wait for the next one!"

—**Susan Alpert,** PhD, MD, Microbiologist, Pediatrician, Founder and Principal, SFA Regulatory, LLC, Former Corporate Senior Vice President for Global Regulatory at Medtronic

"*Getting to G.R.E.A.T.* is a gift to the cluttered mind. Through stories and research, Madelaine takes on the swirl of purpose, ambition, meaning, and fear that fills up our minds—and offers a simple path for sorting it all out."

—**Brett Jenks,** President and CEO, Rare, A Global Conservation Organization

"Madelaine Weiss's *Getting to Great* is very well researched and written. It is heartfelt, engaging, and full of helpful insights, observations, and recommendations."

—**Edward Segal,** Crisis Management Expert, Author of *Crisis Ahead: 101 Ways to Prepare for and Bounce Back from Disasters, Scandals, and Other Emergencies*

"*Getting to Great* is a deep dive into life, revealing not just how and why we are wired, but how and why we wire ourselves. This new work is warm and insightful, rooted in science, and brimming with real-life stories, friendly exercises, and a generous dose of follow-up resources. Madelaine Weiss delivers a wise and witty game plan for nailing happiness and success in work and life. An eye-opening read!"

—Madelyn R. Appelbaum, Co-author of *Stress-Free Performance Appraisals*

"In *Getting to G.R.E.A.T.*, Madelaine Weiss provides readers with a valuable service: demonstrating how to move from thinking and contemplation to action and results. The approach, based on her extensive educational and professional background, illuminates a holistic path to success inside and outside the workplace."

—Bruce Rosenstein, MLS, Author of *Create Your Future the Peter Drucker Way* and *Living in More Than One World*

"*Getting to G.R.E.A.T.* is the kind of book that offers some truly practical information, based in scientific reasoning and easy to carry out. It is creatively grounded and explorative at the same time. As a person who owns my own healthcare business, in these stressful times, I intend to recommend this book to my coworkers, to my friends, and to my employees."

—Judy Carney, MPA, Health and Healthy Lifestyle Specialist and CEO of Network Therapies

"*Getting to Great* is a one-of-a-kind book. Madelaine Weiss makes an intimate connection with her readers as she explains the 'why' and 'how' of our thoughts influence our life choices. She passionately shares examples of lives in and out of balance and provides exercises to help us recognize, explore and tackle the challenges stopping us from achieving our work/life quality. A must read!"

—Al Lichtenstein, HR Consultant and Coach, HR Results, LLC

"Madelaine Weiss's *Getting to Great: A Five Step Strategy for Work and Life* is an outstanding book needed more now than ever. Her ability to blend what science tells us with real stories of real people drives her point home magnificently—you have to fit who you are with the environment that best fits you. *Getting to Great* is a refreshing, uplifting, and inspirational book you should read if you truly want lifelong happiness!"

—**Frank DiBartolomeo,** President of DiBartolomeo Consulting International (DCI), LLC, and Author of *Speak Well and Prosper*

"Madelaine Weiss has made a wonderful contribution to improving how we approach work, life, and happiness (however we wish to define it)!! While there are plenty of 'How Best to Be Successful' books out there, Madelaine's discussion is straightforward and powerful, captured in five steps. *Getting to G.R.E.A.T.* is a must read, and you will find yourself giving copies away to others who can benefit from the wisdom and results offered within its pages.

—**Jack L. Gates,** Founding Director of Leadership Breakfast Maryland, former President of the National Captioning Institute

"Madelaine Weiss shares with us her genius in *Getting to G.R.E.A.T.* She starts with real-life stories, some heart-wrenching, as a baseline to help you explore—through case studies, science, and then exercises—how you indeed can be the G.R.E.A.T. you want. Madelaine takes us on a journey of discovery, and you can jump in at any point to try some of the exercises she suggests to enjoy the life you want to lead. No matter where you are in your career or life, soak up some of Madelaine's wisdom. I wish I had this book as a young working mom, later at mid-career, and finally as a reference as a seasoned senior executive."

—**Wendy King,** Leadership Expert, Author of *Avoid the Pitfalls,* and former CFO, West Virginia University Health Sciences Center

"*Getting to Great* is the go-to book on how work affects our everyday lives and what to do about it. It provides real-life tips, tools, and solutions to live a happier, healthier, and more productive life. If you want a roadmap for a more joyful life, this book is for you."

—**Arnold Sanow,** MBA, CSP, Speaker and Author of *Get Along with Anyone, Anytime, Anywhere*

Getting to G.R.E.A.T.

*A 5-Step Strategy For Work and Life
Based on Science and Stories*

By Madelaine Claire Weiss

Published by

◤ köehlerbooks™

3705 Shore Drive
Virginia Beach, VA 23455
800–435–4811
www.koehlerbooks.com

GETTING TO
G.R.E.A.T.

A 5-STEP STRATEGY FOR WORK AND LIFE

BASED ON SCIENCE AND STORIES

MADELAINE CLAIRE WEISS

VIRGINIA BEACH
CAPE CHARLES

This book is dedicated to

My dear, departed father,
who cared so much and tried so hard,
My children and grandchildren,
Marlyn, Marshall, Sam, Marisa, Laila,
Joseph, Francesca, Gabriella, George,
for making my heart burst with love and pride,
and
Grandmom Rose for always being there. Sort of.

TABLE OF CONTENTS

INTRODUCTION
WHY THIS MATTERS

A GREAT LIFE depends on a great fit between who we are and the environments in which we work and live. Otherwise, we are not only unhappy but, like fish out of water, potentially worse. My father was a business owner who died at forty-two years old. I was fifteen. The doctor said he died of a cerebral hemorrhage, but since I was grounded at the time for speaking truth to power *again,* I was pretty sure he died of me. It was not until one day at the cemetery, when I finally broke down with my mother about how "all my fault" it was, that I found out it was not me after all. In her shining moment as a mom, she said tenderly, "No, honey, it wasn't you. It was work."

The Japanese have a word for it: *karoshi,* death by overwork—sometimes by suicide, heart attack, or stroke. In my dad's case, it was stroke. It may have been a simple biological event waiting to happen or, okay fine, maybe a little bit of me, or maybe it really was death by overwork. He did go into work at 5 a.m. and not come home until around 10 p.m. every day except Sunday, when he went in at 5 a.m. and came home around noon.

Whatever it was, helpless and useless I watched him lie comatose in the hospital bed, guiding the bedsheets between his fingers through an imaginary sewing machine. So even if it was not work that killed him, it is fair to say the man worked until his dying breath, and would have done it no other way. That's just what he did, and a little later we will talk about why, because it could apply to you or someone you love. A lot of people work too much—harder, not smarter, as we say today.

Some statistics:

- Forbes reports the US to be the most overworked nation in the developed world.[1]

- Global Organization for Stress reports work-stress levels rising around the world.[2]

- American Institute of Stress reports 94 percent of American workers experience work stress.[3]

- *Washington Post* reports work stress to be among the top five causes of death.[4]

The physical, emotional, and behavioral symptoms are exhaustive, frightening, and too often ignored or blamed on someone or something else. But more and more people—employers, employees, entrepreneurs—are realizing that even before Covid-19, there was something about work that has adversely affected every inch of their lives. Now more than ever they know that either being or having people around us who are the wrong people in the wrong place in the wrong way eventually brings everyone down. It is depressing, demoralizing, and good for no one's bottom line. And they want to fix it, but try as they might, they don't know how. So the coaching industry has been exploding.[5]

Nearly all of my clients these days come to me about work. Still, everything is connected to everything else, so at their request, we work on their health, their money, their relationships with spouses, kids, parents, and their challenges external to work. They are who they are wherever they go, so gains they make in one part of their lives affect other parts too, much to their surprise and delight. Yes, even in troubled times, we are capable of delight. And it is a privilege and a pleasure for me to be a part of it all.

It is also not rocket science that I would wind up helping working people live happier, healthier, more productive lives for the benefit of themselves and all the (big and little) people counting on them, remembering the nothing I could do then to make a difference for my dad's work stress. Clearly, I love this work because it works, because it makes a difference, and because it is simply the absolutely perfect environmental fit for me. We will be talking more about environmental fit, among other ways of thinking and doing that can make a difference for you, no matter the circumstances around you.

Yes indeed, there are things we can do, actions we can take, to find or create an environment we want to live in, the way we want to live in it. Or at least to get closer than you may have thought possible. Some of my clients have switched companies or industries. One decided to stick with the work and improved his environmental fit by moving to a new home he finally loves. Another, down-and-out bored at work and afraid she would never want to live with another person, is now living happily on the other side of the country with a husband and a job filled with promotions and opportunities to keep her growing and stimulated for now and the foreseeable future.

Numbers of talented men, paralyzed by career indecision, came alive when they realized that they could have and do it all to their hearts content over time, one step at a time. One picked up his family and moved to New Zealand to practice his craft on the other side of the world. And then, and this is important, there are the many, many others who reset their internal environment and fell in love with exactly where they are.

As different as these people are from each other, and no matter how the world changes, they get to great in work and life with the same five-step strategy:

- *Grounding* in the belief that a great life is possible— through a great environmental fit.

- *Recognizing* that fitness begins with and requires knowing who we are—our internal environment.

- *Exploring* out-of-the-box alternatives and possibilities—our external environment.

- *Acting* on a new environmental vision—because there is no success without action.

- *Tackling* the mind's normal, natural resistance to change—so it doesn't get in the way.

All of these clients have done this *grounding, recognizing, exploring, acting, tackling* to improve their environmental fit. And this is not new, dear reader. The world has changed before. And we know from Darwin that the organisms that fit best with their environments are the ones most likely to survive and to thrive. Why does this matter? Because too many families suffer needlessly, and because hundreds of billions of dollars are lost due to absenteeism, poor performance, and illness caused by high stress and boredom associated with poor fit on the job.[6] Since everything is connected to everything else—employers, employees, entrepreneurs—all feel the pain. *And it does not have to be this way.* It is my hope that you will find, between these pages, that some of what has worked for others will help you get to thinking, being, feeling, and doing *great* in your work and life too, no matter what.

Notes

The stories in this book are, when not specified otherwise, the stories of real individuals I have known personally or professionally. To respect their privacy, I have changed their names and other identifying information.

The information provided in this book is designed to provide helpful information on the subjects discussed. This book is not meant to be used, nor should it be used, to diagnose or treat any medical, emotional, or mental health condition. For diagnosis or treatment of any medical, emotional, or mental health problem, please consult your physician.

PART I:
GETTING TO GREAT AT WORK

> Our deeds determine us,
> as much as we determine our deeds.
> ~ *George Eliot*

1
WHO ARE WE? WHO ARE YOU?

The Hard Question

MOST KIDS GO OUT TO PLAY. Some kids aren't allowed. I talked back to my mom and dad too much, so I was *never* allowed out, or that's how I remember it anyway. Take the time my mother and I were having a whispering discussion about my teenage smoking. This was late at night by *her* side of *their* bed. I am not sure why we were not at *my* side of *my* bed, since I am pretty sure I went in there to discuss my trouble sleeping and got a smoking-cessation lecture instead. In any case, I wrapped it up with a little whispering of my own: "Well, I never said I didn't smoke; I just never said I did." Ha!

I have to admit I figured that the real power was asleep next to her in the bed, only he wasn't asleep enough. That little encounter was good for another two weeks in the slammer while the whole rest of the world was out playing. Now, you might think that the consequences of my behavior would have helped me to put a lid on it. That's what my older brother did. But no. I wanted to be accepted for who I was, or at least for my favorite version of who I was—the brave, courageous, and bold one, just like the spirited one in the children's book *Madeline*. And the only way you can know that you are being accepted for who you are is to *be* who you are and let the chips fall where they may.

"I want to be accepted for who I am" is a common refrain, a common yearning. And, of course, different people play it out differently. So when a colleague, Sarah, said it to me, I asked her, "So, who is this who wants to be accepted for who she is? Who are you, Sarah?" And she was stumped. No matter how hard Sarah tried, on each try, she defined herself by what she had done. Roles played. Missions accomplished. Sarah could say she was a lawyer, a teacher, an author, a board member, a mother, a wife—none of which felt to her like who she wanted to be accepted as.

Finally, Sarah said she is someone who wants to contribute to make the world a better place. And when asked, "Why is that?" she did not know. In all fairness to Sarah, much of what makes us tick is unconscious. As Nobel Prize–winning psychologist Daniel Kahneman put it, "You may not know that you are optimistic about a project because something about its leader reminds you of your beloved sister, or that you dislike a person who looks vaguely like your dentist."[7]

Think about it. How could our brain possibly keep conscious all of the information thrown at it by the eyes, nose, ears, tongue, and skin? These sense organs send about eleven million bits of information per second to the brain for processing, but the conscious mind handles only about fifty bits per second of it.[8] This stunning gap between what is and our severely limited conscious awareness of what is should make us question how we think we know anything at all. Let alone anything about who or what we are in this vast universe of ours. So then, who is this thing called "mind" who thinks it knows so much when really it knows so little? Don't worry if you can't answer that question. Most people can't.

This is probably why philosophers and neuroscientists call the question of human consciousness the "the hard question."[9] To give that some perspective, I once attended an exhibit on "BRAIN" at the Museum of Science in Boston. A good exhibit, I thought—lots of pamphlets on what the brain looks like and what we think we know to date about how it works. On the way out, I stopped to thank the nice young woman at the reception table. I also had a question for her: "I notice the word *mind* is used a lot, but I couldn't find a definition anywhere in your exhibit. Can you tell me please what *mind* is?" Not even flustered, she said, "Oh, yes, well, we don't really know what that is; that's why there is no definition." Not a great answer, so the question remains.

Who Is Mind?

The brain and the mind. Are they the same thing or something different? Are they even things at all or something else entirely? This is not a new question. Remember Descartes: *I think, therefore I am.*

I believe what Descartes meant was that after he got finished doubting the existence of everything he could think of to doubt, still left standing was the one doing the doubting. For Descartes, the mind was a "thinking thing."[10] Still, who or what exactly is the "thinking thing"? Not too long ago I asked a Harvard cognitive development professor,

"You seem to be using brain and mind interchangeably as if there is no distinction. Can you please comment on that?" He snapped back, "Let me put it to you this way: if you take a brain out and slice it up, what do you think will be left of the mind?" Well then, why use two different words? I didn't think his answer was helpful, so I ran it by a philosopher, who called him a materialist.

Nonmaterialists have a different way of thinking about the *Who am I?* question. Advaita Vedanta pre-Hindu tradition[11] holds that "one cannot be that which one observes. I am not this body." Advaita Vedantists also do not think that we are the mind. Who or what is doing the thinking, and who or what is observing the thing that is doing the thinking? We know when the thinking thing is thinking. So who is doing the knowing? There has to be something else. It can get a little "out there" in every direction. For example, Deepak Chopra refers to the something else as "spirit[,] . . . the consciousness of immortality in the midst of mortality."[12] At the other end of the spectrum, we have mind as machine.

We already know that machines can bury us at chess, but what if machines could learn how to interpret body language and follow eye movements? What if we understood that computers are already prostheses for the brain? This is what Pierre Baldi meant by wetware (brain) and hardware (machine), when he predicted that the entire contents of a brain would someday be "storable inside the memory of a single computer."[13] It is what *Wired* magazine's Kevin Kelly meant, in 1994, when he predicted "the whole world networked into a human/machine mind."[14] Well then, that future is now. And where am I right now? I am with my computer and my iPhone, through which almost all of my research and correspondence about work and play take place. My neuro-psycho-social-cyber network: *I compute, therefore I am.*

I am my computer. Computer-I-am. So, now what is mind? And who or what am I? From cognitive psychologist Steven Pinker: "The mind is a system of organs of computation, designed by natural selection to solve the kinds of problems our ancestors faced in their foraging way of life, in particular, understanding and outmaneuvering objects, animals, plants, and other people. . . . [M]ind is what the brain does. . . . [T]he brain processes information, and thinking is a kind of computation."[15]

That's a kind of mind-as-machine interpretation too, although Pinker wanted us to know that the mind can work like a machine without being a machine, just as an eye can work like a camera without being a camera.[16] So, we are not really machines. Phew. But he did say mind is what brain does. We are what we do. And in this we are all very much alike.

How Are We Alike?

Humans are all wired up for problem-solving. This is why, even though I am licensed to do so, I do not refer to my clients as patients and do not diagnose them clinically. Roman emperor and philosopher Marcus Aurelius said, "Life is what our thoughts make it."

Today we say it's all in how we frame it. And we do get to frame it. So, I do not frame the work we do as about illness. It is, rather, about strategy. Where do you want to go in your life? How have you been trying to get there? What is working? What is not working? What could work even better? And what's in the way? Though humans around the world may appear different in size, shape, and color, we are 99.9 percent alike genetically, all peas in a pod trying to get through the day in the best ways we know how. All of us driven to survive—and to thrive. The tree wants to grow. The bird wants to fly. And so do we.

Some of the underlying forces we have in common are considered basic human drives. From Lawrence and Nohria, in their book *Driven*: "One of the innate drives located in the minds of all humans is the drive to acquire . . . to seek, take, control, and retain objects and personal experiences humans value. . . . [H]umans who achieve relative success in acquiring have literally and figuratively better survival prospects."[17]

These authors address other basic drives too, including the drive to bond, drive to learn, and drive to defend. In *Beyond Reason,* Fisher and Shapiro list appreciation, affiliations, autonomy, status, and role fulfillment as aspects of life and living we all care about.[18] And in *Paradoxes of Group Life,*[19] Smith and Berg include belonging, engaging, speaking, scarcity, perception, and power. Life is complicated, so I like to look for the common denominator: the thing that most affects everything else. To bond, to learn, affiliations, autonomy, status, role, belonging, engaging, speaking. A full read of each text suggests a common human tension in pursuit of an individual identity—a drive to be different—as we also endeavor to belong.

How Are We Different?

The nature-versus-nurture debate is a gigantic, well-researched subject, so we are not going into the weeds on it here. For our purposes, suffice it to say that last I checked, there appears to be general agreement that it is both nature and nurture that makes us who we are.[20] Genes do not dictate who we are. It is the expression of our genes, depending on the life we live, that makes me "me" and you "you." And now hear this because it is what this book is about: *It is possible to change the "what is" to "what could become" for each and every one of us.*

Psychologists claim that personality can change.[21] Although this does mean that some people who used to fit into our lives might not fit anymore, this is still incredibly good news for anyone wishing to up-level the fulfillment in their lives. Sometimes a change in how we are in the world is due to the impact of unfortunate circumstances. Sometimes it is due to an intentional effort of our own, often including people who see the best in us before we can see it in ourselves. This is that **grounding** in the belief that great things are possible with the proper support—the first phase of work for my clients who transform their lives.

In *The Moral Animal,* Robert Wright calls it knobs and tunings. The "basic knobs of human nature" are capacities we all have to one extent or another; capacities for "love, lust, compassion, reverence, ambition, anger, fear, pangs of conscience, of guilt, of obligation, of shame, and so on."[22] Tunings are why one of us might be more dialed up on lust, ambition, compassion, etc., than another person. This is how we can be different. This is also how we can change. According to Wright, tunings that are different from others', even different over time from our former selves' tunings, are due to interaction between our social environment and the assets/liabilities we each bring to that environment.

Take Darlene. Darlene is one of the most well-informed people I know, *about everything*: trees, shrubs, food, wine, finance, medicine, politics, childcare, education, dressmaking, decorating, global warming, you name it. Darlene has a master's degree, and even though her children are grown and out of the home, Darlene has never and still does not want to "work outside the home." As the eldest of six children, she feels she "worked" her entire childhood, and then while raising her own family. So now, although she cooks for the hungry through her church and runs a committee where she lives, she has no interest in doing anything that she would consider "work."

For an example of a different tuning, given common knobs, I cannot imagine ever not working. At fifteen-plus years old, one day after school I went into every storefront in our neighborhood, filling out applications, trying to get a job. Because no one hired me and no one told me why, I always imagined that my mother went in behind me to tell them that we would be okay. Possibly because he was young and not expecting to die, my father left us very little money. So my mom took a job in a steel factory right after he died. And I wanted to help. Just as Darlene's environment left her not wanting to do paid work outside the home, mine left me grateful every day for the privilege to do both volunteer and pair work outside the home, and never wanting to stop.

Who Is in Charge?

Work means a lot to a lot of us. Gallup found consistently (from 1989 to 2014) that roughly 55 percent of American workers get their sense of identity from their work.[23] My brother recalls that our dad really enjoyed the feeling of accomplishment. But I knew it was more. I knew that when my father's mom lay dying, he made a deathbed promise that he would take care of his father and keep the family business alive. Hence the incredibly long work hours and an over-the-top devotion to his dad. It was an attachment to a "good son" identity that had him working until his dying breath, fingers pushing the hospital bedsheets through his imaginary sewing machine. It was an attachment to an identity that may have contributed to his death.

Nonetheless, it is how my father gave meaning and

purpose to his life. It became who he was. We are what we do. And we do what we are. Journalist Derek Thompson calls it "workism," meaning that, here in the US especially, work has become the "centerpiece of one's identity and life's purpose."[24] The original purpose of work was to create and provide goods and services, tools and techniques necessary for human survival—food, clothing, shelter, and so on. What was wrong with that? Why can't we do what's necessary and be done for the day?

Well, for one thing, maybe because we have largely met these basic needs as a species, higher-order needs are now driving the bus. It is also the case that a lot of people say they are just plain bored. They think that is because their work lacks meaning and purpose, rather than because the brain likes novelty and simply gets bored doing the same ole same ole, no matter how noble the cause. Nothing wrong with being bored. Nothing we can't fix. But let's not blame it on the work, per se. New things—jobs, people, cars, toys—give us a dopamine rush in anticipation of reward.[25] It is exciting. It feels good. And it wears off as soon as what was new is not new anymore. But that is not the only way to get that rush we humans like. Dominance is another way to get a rush. So, if vervet monkeys and college fraternity presidents get serotonin rushes when they ascend to alpha status,[26] no wonder no matter where they are in the ladder, a lot of folks just want to ascend. Because it feels good. And because it feels good, it feels right.

But just because it feels good does not make it right. In fact, the advice to "follow your passion" can steer you dead wrong. Cynthia, a lawyer who was raised by an overly authoritarian, abusive father, would tell you herself that she is driven passionately to defend the defenseless against authority. Too often, because Cynthia is driven by her passion, she blindly pushes the ethics envelope, telling herself it is okay because of her deeply felt sense that she is on the side of right. This results in Cynthia having to spend time and energy defending her own conduct, time and energy she could spend generating more clients and revenue, which is what her conscious mind thinks she wants.

Cynthia is now countering the real demon: the hungry, out-of-control ego currently in charge. Freud's ego is a part of us all, there to protect, preserve, mediate, and navigate a more-or-less fragile sense of "I exist in this world." On some level we all know that there was a time before we were born when we did not exist and there will be a time once we die when we will not exist again. Reassuring us of our existence in the face of certain nonexistence is a very big job—too big, sometimes. And the ego needs our help so it doesn't run out of control.

Case Example

Carol felt somewhere between stuck and despairing at a company where she believed she would never be able to ascend the way her ego wanted her to without wrecking her family life.

After **grounding** with me in the belief that a great life is possible for her, Carol **recognized** that she needed to knowwhat mattered most to her before she could find her fit and her smile. An inventory of her life values, coupled with her Covid-related "work from home" experience, brought how much family mattered to her into sharp awareness. Carol began **exploring** alternative environments, e.g., companies with family-friendlier cultures, and then began **acting** on interviews and negotiations with a company she was really excited about. To be sure that she did not fall prey to the lure of "the grass is greener," she talked with her present employer about what kind of environmental shifts might possible there as well, and the future is bright. Carol reports that she, her husband, and their daughter are all in very good places: peaceful, optimistic, and joyful. Carol is **tackling** the ego's resistance, the worries and what-ifs, with the reassurance that she's got this now. Because she is shooting now from a clearer, healthier internal environment, she knows she will come out better than okay, no matter where, no matter what. Step by step, one foot in front of the other, Carol is *Getting to Great in Work and Life.*

Next we are a going to dig deeper into the importance of the environmental fit, a fit that, as Carol's story suggests, is possible only once we know who we are. So here is an online life-values inventory tool: https://www.lifevaluesinventory. org. And here below is a mindset exercise to get your wheels turning on that question: *"Who Am I?"*

Exercise:
Who Am I?

You are not your ego. Your ego is a construct of the unconscious mind, there to reassure you, relentlessly, that you exist and that you matter. Because the ego's business is largely unconscious, it practically bullies you into a life story that is not necessarily your conscious choice. But just as a movie may lose some of its impact after you've seen it for the eighth time, so too may your ego's stories on who you should be and how you should live your life.

This exercise is designed to help you replace mindless ego activity with clear and conscious life choices—to create space for your own true needs, values, goals and dreams—by naming and taming the ego events of the mind.

To Practice:

- Sit comfortably in a chair, eyes closed, or simply gaze downward, feet flat on the ground, back nice and straight.

- Begin to breathe gently through your nose. Become aware of your breathing.

- When thoughts occur, note them, and keep them with you long enough for them to expand into the little drama they can become.

- You have now produced and directed a movie of the mind. Give it a title, note the title, let it go, and return your attention to your breathing.

- You may stay in "the movie room" long enough, or repeat the exercise often enough, for you to develop a neutral "Oh, I already saw that" response to the recurrent dramas of your mind. This can set you free to be who you are.

- You may then imagine a different, more aspirational drama about the "you" you want to be in the world. In this version, who do you see? What do you hear? How does it feel? Be as detailed as possible, to bring this "you" alive.

We cannot think of being acceptable to others
until we have first proven acceptable to ourselves.
~ *Malcolm X*

2
ENVIRONMENTAL (MIS)FIT

Impostorism

WE ALL HAVE A SENSE of where we do and do not fit in. We can feel it the minute a plane lands and everyone is speaking a language we do not understand. Or when the plane lands on the other side of the world among people who share our ancestry, so we feel we are with family even though we do not know a soul there. Decisions about where we do and do not fit in shape our lives. But they are not necessarily conscious. This can be a problem.

Years ago, I turned down an acceptance to Harvard for a PhD, telling myself that it would be too hard on my family. Since I already had the husband and my daughter when I applied, if that's how I felt, why did I even apply? And surely there are lots of women who would have gone and made it work, including the woman I am today. Then, when it was time for business school, an esteemed Harvard

Business School professor told my equally esteemed father-in-law, "Tell her to apply; we are looking for people like her." I might have been a shoo-in but did not apply.

Clancy Martin[27] writes that early family dynamics and sex-role stereotypes have resulted in many high-achieving women feeling like impostors. He calls it "impostorism" and says this applies to ethnic minorities as well. There is also, for men and women, something about surpassing one's parents that can make one feel like a fraud. He talks about how hard it is to reality-test performance in the intangible service professions of today, and how comparisons with inflated Facebook posts are not helping either.

Do look at the article if you think it might apply to you or someone you know. After I read it, all of a sudden I thought, *OMG. OMG.* I did have humble beginnings, and I was a girl. Maybe the truth is that I did not think I fit in at Harvard—certainly not for a PhD, an MBA, or anything of the kind. And maybe I thought they made a mistake, just as the author said. I do remember when the professor called my home to tell me that I got accepted. I replied, "Oh, come on, who is this? That's not funny; cut it out." True story.

Meanwhile, the kids turned out great, and I went into other programs anyway. So, hard to know for sure, but chances are I could have made at least one of those programs work. I did make it up to myself a little bit with two clinical placements through the Harvard system. I also worked there for thirteen years, have taken continuing-education courses there, too many to count, and I absolutely love my work now. But that's not the point. The point here is that false selves, inflated or deflated, can never be fulfilled because they do not exist. They are false. And because they are false, they do not even fit in with themselves, let alone with anyone anywhere else. As before, absent a good enough fit with the environment—internal and external—we are in trouble.

Internal Environment

To be clear, the person–environment fit can be complicated because we all have an internal environment, an external environment, and multiple levels of each. Martin's point, if I read him right, is that there are so many reasons (emotional, psychological, social, cultural, etc.) for us to doubt ourselves that we should probably worry more about the people who don't. As in, what kind of arrogance or departure from reality does it take for someone not to doubt whether they have what it takes to succeed where they have never been before—especially in the context of messages that one does not belong there anyway? So, the internal signals mean well. For one thing, they are there to protect us from making fools out of ourselves. And the stronger the signals are, the more automatically we think they must be right.

Wrong. We have to consider the signals carefully, *especially* because they are that strong. We have to read and apply them, or overrule them, as correctly as we can, so they do not lead us astray through the strength of their brute force. Self-limiting thoughts can become habits of the mind that greatly impact the direction of our lives. Joseph Grenny's study of 1,000 managers found that 97 percent had at least one career-limiting habit (CLH):[28]

1. Unreliability
2. "It's not my job"
3. Procrastination
4. Resistance to change
5. Negative attitude

The career-limiting habit can be seen as a strategy to keep us safe. So even when the managers knew about their CLH, many clung to it for dear life anyway, hoping their strengths would compensate. Strengths do compensate, but only to a point. And, oh, by the way, it is not hard to see how items 1 through 5 above can serve as what I am calling relationship-limiting habits (RLHs), too. You can see how the complex internal environment plays a pivotal role in environmental fit, and the life we lead associated with it.

Grenny suggests numbers of ways to begin modifying these self-limiting internal habits of the mind. One is to take a brave and bold visit to your "default future." That is, who, what, and where do you think you will wind up—if you do not change your CLH (or RLH)? He actually does a monetary calculation of lost income due to lost promotions caused by, let's just say, inartful behavior. So, why didn't the 97 percent just give it up? Because it's not that simple. As before, we are barely aware of all that really drives us deep down. Welcome to mismatch theory.

External Environment

"Mismatch theory" in human affairs is based on the idea that we possess traits (including behavioral patterns) that have been preserved by natural selection because of their adaptive function in a specific environment—which for most of our evolutionary history was *very* unlike that in which we now find ourselves. Our ancient adaptive traits are thus frequently mismatched to the current environment—and thus we find ourselves doing the best we can to deal with contemporary stimuli using the traits we *do* possess.[29]

In short, evolutionary psychology's *"mismatch hypothesis"* is that human behavior traits were formed in the environment of evolutionary adaptation (EEA) about 125,000 years ago and are therefore mismatched to the actual environment we live and work in today. However, the hypothesis is not without its critique. Arguments against, most notably from the late paleontologist Stephen Jay Gould,[30] center on the difficulty in disentangling biology and culture—that, plus the abundance of studies on American college students, as if college students are somehow representative of all *Homo sapiens.*

Still, the mismatch hypothesis holds that we were not built for demands on minds and bodies that were developed at an earlier time for other things. Mismatches are everywhere. Even at—especially at—work. In *Evolution in the Office,*[31] the authors talk about how dramatically different our modern-day office environment is from the savanna-type environment for which our brains have been adapted. Their premise is that the modern-day office causes biophilia, a longing for our natural environment. So, for example, they recommend an external environment with windows for sunlight, actual greenery, or images of greenery, napping times and places, and both exercise and socialization opportunities.

Now, some would say, please . . . those office windows have nothing at all to do with our love of and yearning for sunlight. It's cultural, not biological. An office with a window is all about prestige. Well, guess what? Some would say that prestige, or status seeking, is biologically programmed into who we are too. Let's hear again from one of my favorites, Robert Wright, who wrote the book I cut my teeth on after hearing him speak at a small seminar I attended back in the '90s. From his book, *The Moral Animal*:

> The stakes are very real. Resources are allotted in rough accordance with status. . . . The genes may

work by instilling drives that, in humans, get labeled "ambition" or "competitiveness"; or by instilling feelings such as "shame" (along with an aversion to it and a tendency to feel it after conspicuous failure); or "pride" (along with an attraction to it and a tendency to feel it after doing impressive things). But whatever the exact feelings, if they raise fitness, they will become part of the species' psychology. . . . Whether we know it or not, we tend naturally to rank one another, and we signify that rank through patterns of attention, agreement, and deference—whom we pay attention to, whom we agree with, whose jokes we laugh at, whose suggestions we take. [32]

Status matters, more than we think it should, and my clients tell the tale. Otherwise wonderfully attractive and talented men and women, they are restricted in work and love *by their own condemnation of the very human nature that Wright just described*. Whether we know it or not, whether we like it or not, the best of us can experience ambition, competitiveness, shame, pride, envy, jealously. These are human qualities that may have helped us to survive and to thrive as a species, even if they are at times overblown, overdone, and overused in our present-day environment.

Little do we know, in the way that we need to know, that if someone else appears to have more status than we do ourselves, we will not be deprived of food and drink and left to die. That is not the kind of external environment we live in anymore. We may feel bummed. But we will not die. And it is a serious case of "mismatch" to respond as if we will. We may be programmed to feel crummy if we have tried in work or love and missed our mark. We are wired for this, from a long, long, time ago when the stakes were a whole lot higher than they are today. Okay, fine, we may want to lay low (get depressed) for a limited period of time so no further shame nor harm comes our way until we feel better enough to try again. Still, we will not die. But the brain is not convinced, so it makes us feel, think, and behave as if we will. When all we really need to do is take Tylenol.

Not kidding. Studies show that social pain hurts as much or more than physical pain, and lives in the same part of the brain as physical pain as well.[33] You know (or if not, try this and see) that you have a harder time vividly reexperiencing a physical pain than reexperiencing the social pain you feel at the thought or sight, let's say, of the one who rejected you in love. And it hardly even matters who did the rejecting. The team that didn't want you, the job you didn't get, the old love you see with his/her new love, the person who snubbed you on the street—it all hurts from the same part of the brain as physical pain and can therefore be treated as such. Tylenol. So what's all this social fuss about?

The answer lies in our evolutionary past. Humans are social animals; being rejected from our tribe or social group in our pre-civilized past would have meant losing access to food, protection, and mating partners, making it extremely difficult to survive. Being ostracized would have been akin to receiving a death sentence. Because the consequences of ostracism were so extreme, our brains developed an early-warning system to alert us when we were at risk for being "voted off the island" by triggering sharp pain whenever we experienced even a hint of social rejection.

Take the ball-tossing scenario.[34] It goes something like this: Three people (two researchers, one subject) are sitting in a waiting room. One researcher starts tossing a ball to another, which goes around evenly among the three of them until the second round, when they skip passing it to the subject. As silly as it sounds, dozens of studies have shown that a rejection this mild can cause mood and self-esteem-altering emotional pain. And that was nothing. They were total strangers in a waiting room, so it makes sense how much more painful social rejection can be where it might matter a bit if not a lot more. You know that party you didn't even want to go to, and still you felt bad that you didn't make the cut? Or that meeting, or the memo you didn't get. Who cares? We do because, like it or not, the brain is wired to care. It happens to the best of us.

Some get it worse than others. The brain's natural pain-killing response (μ-opioid, morphine) varies among us.[35] And believe it or not, some personality types seem even to thrive on social rejection. For example, one study found that some independent types may take social rejection as a validation of their specialness, inspiring creativity and productivity—contrasted with other types in whom a lowering of cognitive functioning during the post-rejection phase has been found. The fear of social pain is so great for a number of clients that they are willing to constrict their lives severely in work, play, and love to keep themselves feeling safe.[36] On the other hand, they did reach out, so good for them for knowing there must be a happier, healthier, more productive way to live their lives, if they can learn to modulate the pain.

There are, of course, ways other than Tylenol to deal with life-limiting reactions to social pain. One is to watch out for how we talk to ourselves about it. Try this: Welcome to the human race. It's normal. It's okay. It has happened to the best of us. You are not the first and you will not be the last to suffer rejection. The pain of it all has helped us to survive and thrive as a species, so it is not going away anytime soon. And it does have an upside. For one, rejection is an opportunity to get some feedback on how we are seen in the world, just in case there is something we might want to tweak. Rejection also provides data that we can use to discern who and what may be a good environmental fit, and who or what may not. The idea is to get off the sofa, ask yourself what, if anything, there is to learn, and then get back out there among the living to fully live your life.

Above all, remember that the pain of external-environment rejection is fueled by an age-old fear of dying as a result of not belonging, and not being seen as good enough to receive care and resources from our kin. You might be surprised—I know I was—at how many and what kinds of people care more than anything about being seen as good. Here is a story about a CEO one would never have suspected of caring about looking good, for all the arrogance he displayed on his surface.

When I was working at Harvard Medical School, I designed and delivered a workshop called "*Organizational Politics: Theory and Practice, Practice, Practice*" for the Center for Workplace Learning and Performance. One of the program's exercises is the *5 Whys*. This exercise is credited to Toyota, but dates all the way back to Aristotle's *Nicomachean Ethics*, around 340 BC. The idea is that asking "why" after the answer to the first question, and then asking "why" after each subsequent answer, will lead us to a root-cause understanding of who we are and why we do what we do. Here below is the case illustration. I am the questioner.

The 5 Whys and the Sleepy, Grumpy CEO

Q1: Why does it bother you so much that your adversary is not on board?

A1: Because I am wasting so much energy trying to bring him on board.

Q2: Why do you need to stop wasting energy trying to bring him on board?

A2: Because I could use that energy to move the project along. (Now the very grumpy CEO is getting annoyed with what seem like stupid questions but persists nonetheless.)

Q3: Why do you need to move the project along?

A3: To fulfill the organization's mission.

Q4: Why do you need to fulfill the organization's mission?

A4: To make everyone happy, even though I know that's not possible.

Q5: Why do you need to make everyone happy?

A5: So I can feel like a good person.

Time after time, person after person, regardless of age and gender, no matter how high up the organizational ladder—the answers were the same. Everyone wanted to be, to feel, and to be seen as a good person. According to Aristotle, the ultimate aim of human behavior is happiness. From an evolutionary perspective, a sixth question, on why people want to feel like good people, could reveal that our own sense of goodness makes us feel happy because it helps us believe that others can see it too, and that makes us feel safe in a world where, on some level, we all know and are terrified that we are going to die. Just not right now, if that's okay. So, reputation counts. We reap what we sow.

But, but, but . . . Guidelines for goodness are not always clear. So many of my clients are searching for these guidelines outside of themselves, only to finding conflicting opinions, none of which feel authentic because they do not come from inside. And if it does not feel authentic, it does not feel good in any way that sticks. After all, who is doing the doing? It is not you. Others find the whole thing so arbitrary that they give up the search altogether, in a rules-don't-apply-to-me kind of way. These, it seems, are the saddest of all, the ones so jaded that they don't even try.

For those who do try and are still searching for guidelines beyond the ones already familiar to them, where can they turn? Who says what good is? Consideration of others could be our guiding light. But then, for example, is it those who spend their time bringing their genius to others, or those who spend their time in more direct charitable contribution to others, who stack up as morally good? Murky as it may be, if we want to be and do good and, in so doing, experience the happiness this brings, where can we find our answers and guidelines? In his essay on *self-reliance*, Emerson asserts, "A man should learn to detect and watch that gleam of light which flashes across his mind from within, more than the lustre of the firmament of bards and sages. Yet he dismisses without notice his thought, because it is his. In every work of genius we recognize our own rejected thoughts: they come back to us with a certain alienated majesty."[37]

That "light which flashes across his mind" is, of course, inside ourselves. And yet, that Emerson has to tell us this at all shows us how much pull there is to look to the external environment for how to live. It is as if we are saying, "Just tell me what to do so I don't have to worry about the dire consequences of getting it wrong and you, whoever you are, kicking me out, left to die." But then, there is no "I" to kick out, there is no "you," and human nature won't put up with that either. So the continuing search for the greatest environmental fit that we can find seems a struggle worth having, as the very foundation of the great life we all want to have.

Internal-External Integration

Well then, how can we reckon who we truly are with what *both the internal and external environments* demand of us? Early on, as children, we figure out a way to deal with life, and the people and circumstances in it. Sometimes there was trouble in the family, and even in the best of families, we still had to figure out how to deal with the schoolyard. Especially today, children are hardly immune to what is going on around them. Child notice and turn their attention to strategy. And since whatever strategy the child comes up with to deal with life seems to work well enough, that strategy sticks. What this could mean is that *you have a five-year-old in charge of your life*.

No doubt adorable, well-meaning, and smart, but a five-year-old nonetheless, bullying your life away. Because that part of us has a whole constellation of neural connections in our brain, it lives on with all kinds of expectations about how things ought to be. I call this disconnection the *misery gap*, the space between the way things are and the way the bossy little five-year-old thinks things ought to be. And the bigger the gap, the bigger the opportunity to create misery for ourselves. Remember, Pinker said the human mind is a problem-solving machine. But sometimes the solver within us is only around five, with a five-year-old's strategy.

It is not that the little ones who live inside of us do not mean well. They do. They mean to protect us from humiliation and harm. But they are not as smart and well developed as we are as adults. They do not have our ranges of experience and expertise, so they keep pulling the same ole tool out of the toolkit, even if it doesn't apply. Just the other day I talked with a seventy-six-year-old man who can't stand the mess on his desk but can't seem to keep up with the cleaning. No surprise, when he was a child his mother nagged him mercilessly about cleaning his room. Well, he showed her! Only now his mother is not around to care one whit about the mess, and he very much does. So a big part of the work my clients and I do is to separate out who they are from all of the internal and external forces upon them, past and present, so they can, as the wiser, older version of themselves, mediate among those forces with more grown-up strategies for happier, healthier, productive lives.

Case Example

Ryan was up for a long-promised promotion. The C-suite he was meant to join was concerned that he might not have what they considered to be the right kind of temperament for a top leadership role. They thought he was "too nice." It turns out that, in reality, Ryan was so frustrated with how the company was being run that his emotion scared even him, and it took just about everything he had to keep his anger from exploding. Consequently, he came off as too passive, "too nice." Over time, Ryan got *grounded* in the belief that there had to be a better way to deal with his legitimate frustration than just hiding it from everyone, including himself. He *recognized* alternative communication strategies available within himself that felt better to him, fit better with the external environment, and therefore worked better too. Ryan also resumed an earlier meditation practice that set him up to express himself calmly, clearly, authentically, and professionally. Neither too nice, nor not nice enough. But just right. He has not only reduced his blood pressure but also believes he has helped himself to be a better husband and father.

The newfound mastery and confidence of Ryan's internal environment led him to **explore** healthier external environments that he thought might fit better with his own deeply held views on best practices for the industry he loves. And Ryan began **acting** on invitations to be in touch that he had received from colleagues he met at conferences. As of this writing, there is an offer in the works, along with other opportunities. Although Ryan's ego is duly flattered, Ryan knows the difference now between himself and his ego. So he is **tackling** the force of the ego's enjoyment of the flattery to make sure the new external environment is aligned with the values he now knows he has, as he looks forward to *Getting to Great in Work and Life*, in this new way.

To help you review or discover your internal driver(s), here is an exercise on "The 5 Whys and You."

Exercise:
The 5 Whys and You

Something tells you that if you could only change or get rid of some person or thing out there, everything would start going just the way you want it to. But what if the problem is more that what you think you want is out of line with what you are really after underneath it all? How could you possibly know what strategy to use to get you there, if you don't really know who you are and where there is?

This exercise is designed to help you discover what you really want so that you can match a suitable strategy to help you bring it about.

To Practice:

What's in Your Way? Refresh your mind with a few slow, deep breaths, and imagine as vividly as possible a situation in which you feel that your goals are being thwarted, usually but not necessarily involving other persons (e.g., it could be a company policy driving you mad). In the space below write a brief description or draw a picture of "the thwart" (I like to call it a thwart).

The Thwart

What Do You Want? Now try to frame your "5 Whys" with greater focus on *your own responses* to the thwart than on the thwart itself. Otherwise you will end up blaming the thwart rather than learning anything useful about yourself. You have probably been there, done that, and would therefore only wind up at the same boring, frustrating dead end that you have visited too many times before. With this tip in mind, begin your first question, e.g., *Why does it bother me so much that . . . (something about the thwart)?* Or *Why do I . . . (in response to the thwart)?*

Q1:

A1:

Q2:

A2:

Q3:

A3:

Q4:

A4:

Q5:

A5:

What Did You Learn That You Can Use Going Forward?
For Example:

1. That maybe you already have what you want on your job. Enjoy!

2. That you do not have what you want, but could get it some other way, through or around the thwart. Does your thwart even know it's a thwart?

3. That what you want is not attainable but that some other just-as-good goal is?

4. That what you want is attainable, just not in the current setting?

5. That you have trouble moving past a focus on blaming the thwart, in which case try again, anytime you like.

> "Hell is other people."
> ~ *Jean Paul Sartre*

3

OTHER PEOPLE: HEAVEN OR HELL

What Sartre Meant

IT IS A COMMON MISPERCEPTION that "Hell is other people" means that other people are hell and we should avoid their toxicity. What Sartre really meant, in his own words, is this: "Into whatever I say about myself someone else's judgment always enters. Into whatever I feel within myself someone else's judgment enters. . . . But that does not at all mean that one cannot have relations with other people. It simply brings out the capital importance of all other people for each one of us."[38]

Philosopher Charles Horton Cooley said it this way: "I am not who you think I am; I am not who I think I am; I am who I think you think I am."[39] Good one. Spot on. We know that feeling, when what we think they think about what we think feels like hell. Some suffer this hell more than others, and some suffer it but won't admit it because they are ashamed to care that much about what other people think. Still, the wiring is there for humans to care about what other people think as if it's a matter of life and death, because back when our modern brains were forming, it *was* life and death.

And it is very much alive and present today. At a conference I attended with hundreds of other people, when the speaker blurted out, "You're all trying to look good, aren't you?" there was an immediate, knowing, uproarious group guffaw. On some level, everybody knows about looking good in the eyes of others—your mother, your father, your friends, coworkers, employees, employers, you name it. Sartre calls it *"the look of the other,"* and we can almost feel it on our skin[40]—the "me" we see in the eyes of others, who we imagine have all kinds of expectations for and judgments about us. Whether real or imagined, it can feel like hell. But not always. Sometimes the look of the other can feel more like heaven. So, before we get into what goes on in organizations that can feel like a living hell, I want to tell you about the heavenly *"look of Grandmom Rose."*

This Is Heaven

There is a lot you can do when you are home alone because you are punished for talking back to your parents. I would dance my heart out, twirling around in the living room, with frequent stops at the big picture of the legendary and deceased Grandmom Rose, who was both in heaven and sitting on top of the TV set. So Grandmom Rose and I talked a lot in my head when I was home alone, which was almost always. She was always there with me, looking pleased to see me, willing to listen, never turning away, never punishing me, never overwhelmed by what I had to say—always with a wise and warm *look* on her face and in her eyes, to help me find myself and my way.

Please know this, if you don't already: Even if it is not always obvious at times, there are a lot of people who really do mean well and really do want to help. There has certainly been a long string of one after another after another of these real and imagined angels in my life, pitching in on the team with Grandmom Rose. And given a dead dad and an anti-intellectual mom, I honestly do not know where I would have been without them. Maybe it is because I needed them that I let them in, and because I let them in, there they were.

As Tolstoy said, "We don't love men so much for the good they have done us as for the good we have done them."[41] I think that's true. An Ohio State study found that people are overwhelmingly motivated to help others even at some cost to themselves.[42] Another study found that cultures around the world rate caring for loved ones as what matters to them most.[43] Don't forget that we all come into the world helpless, so if humans did not evolve equipped to care for others, we would have gone extinct. Pray tell, then, how is it possible that we humans can behave as abominably as we do so much of the time, especially at work?

This Is Hell: Organizational Politics

Treat yourself to one of Hal Hellman's books on people problems in specific occupations, such as medicine, mathematics, technology, or science. I own the medical one. There we find the masters of the mental going mental themselves—namely, Freud and Jung:

> Freud fell over in a dead faint during a discussion
> . . . and Jung carried him to a couch. . . . As with
> many family relationships, this one had elements of
> both love and hate. . . . Freud suggested that he hated
> Jung because of what he perceived as Jung's death

wish toward him. Jung, for his part, commented: "Just like a woman. Confront her with a disagreeable truth: she faints."[44]

You may call it office politics. I don't think we really know what an office is anymore, so I am calling it *organizational politics*, which is what we are going to focus on now. You may already know a lot about it. You know about things like "You scratch my back; I'll scratch yours," "You scratch my back, but then, sorry, I have places to go, people to see, so too bad about you," or "Get off my back; it doesn't look good for me to be hanging out with you." You get the picture. Now, for a more formal definition of organizational politics, I put together for us a composite definition that I like. The first line refers to politics; the second refers to organizations:

- *The "process by which resources are divvied up"*[45]
- *among "a body of persons organized for some specific purpose."*[46]

Why do we divvy? We divvy to survive and to thrive. The story from evolutionary psychology goes something like this: Once upon a time, many millions of years ago, the forest pickings—or resources—were plenty enough for our ancestors to get along just fine. At some point,[47] climate changes shrank the forests and left our apelike ancestors with hardly enough fruits and veggies to pick and to eat. But there was meat, animals all around. We just had to get out there and get them before they got us. Apes who could stand taller on two feet, who could see better, carry things more easily—apes who would develop a brain large enough to permit the design and use of weapons—would prevail. But there was more.

We couldn't just climb up a tree to hide from predators

or get food. There were hardly any trees, and besides, we had to stand our ground, ready to kill at a moment's notice. We also had to take care of each other or we would be meat. So we had to temper aggression within the group. We had to develop roles, rights, responsibilities; we had to divvy up the work and the meat, all of this through communication systems that grew increasingly more complex than our original grunts and cries and gestures—although some of us still like to use gestures. Divvying up resources, roles, rights, responsibilities . . . should sound familiar.

Organizational politics was born and persists with us to this day to help us to survive and to thrive in whatever our own circumstances may be. Let's turn now to a central feature of this expanded, more complicated way of life— territoriality, or "us vs. them."

Territoriality or Us Versus Them

We needed to know who was in and who was out so we knew where to cooperate and where to compete. Because outcasts were met with near-certain death or danger in the ancestral environment—no protection, no food, or worse—we are wired to do everything we can to make sure that we are in. As I said before, you may feel crummy when you don't get an invitation to that party, or your name isn't on the memo for the meeting. You may not even want to go to that party or that meeting, and you feel crummy that you didn't make the cut. Not as stupid as it sounds. Of course we are interested in those territorial boundaries: who's in, who's out, and our place in all of that. It's what makes us feel safe.

We establish strength and security by drawing territorial boundaries and then boundaries within the boundaries. We call that hierarchy—and we draw these lines in our own heads and in the heads of other people through a variety of cooperative and competitive tactics, such as alliance-building, shunning, and the like. Everyone pretty much knows his/her place within the hierarchy. We may not love it, but we can live with it while we work on ways—gathering resources—to climb it, to climb out of it, or at least to get our due compensation and recognition for our support of it. This is organizational politics. It may be politics, but it is our politics, and it has been with us much too long, and served us much too well (we are here, are we not?) for it to be going away anytime soon.

And sometimes we hurt each other deeply when it goes awry, at any and every level of the organization and beyond. Especially when organizations are in decline, workers imagine—and then resent—the C-suite for feeling no pain, which is not necessarily true. Sometimes it is just a "someone to be mad at" who really doesn't need to be poked at unduly while they are throwing everything possible into making things better for all. So, what can we do? Well, for one thing, who puts those us-versus-them territorial boundary lines there in the first place? We do.

So, if we can put the lines there through the sheer power of our minds, then why not use those same powers to relocate or temporarily suspend the lines, even if only for the time it takes to do the work we are meant to do together? This would be similar to when two people come together to have sex. People come together in a little "hot group" at work to get something done, and then throw the walls up again to go about their day or night as individuals when it's over. We do it all the time; we regulate our boundaries. All I am suggesting is that we do it with the smarter, kinder higher brain in charge, so that innocent people don't get hurt (through racism, sexism, ageism, etc.[48]) and good work gets done.

Organizational politics is no more and no less than the

ways in which we aim to survive and to thrive in the face of enormous uncertainty at every level of our existence. When it is good, it is very, very good. We know how to work together for a common good. Our first responders for 9/11 and Covid were as good as it gets. But we are not always good—and when we are bad, we are horrid. Consider "the great intimidators."

The Great Intimidators

Christine Comaford reports in *Forbes* that 75 percent of employees have either been target or witness of bullying in the workplace.[49] Bullying is a big problem with big consequences. For example, the first-thing-in-the-morning cortisol (stress-related) levels for bullied respondents were similar to those found in people with post-traumatic stress disorders.[50] With the silent-treatment types of bullies, you might have no idea what you did wrong and spend all day trying to get something right. These demoralizing behaviors are called microinequities or microaggressions. And then there are the chest thumpers—power freaks to the rest of us, but people of exceptional importance and responsibility to themselves.

A high-demand, low-control job can make us sick.[51] It's not so bad to have someone else taking some of the decision-making load off your back. Decisions can be grueling, and there are many too many of them in the course of a day. So sometimes it is good to just give it up to (that person who thinks s/he is) god—if *you decided* to let this one go and live to fight another day for something that matters more. That's what evolutionary psychiatrist Russell Gardner said: as long as letting it go is voluntary, we can avoid becoming depressed.[52] Of course, companies suffer too, because a lot of victims just leave when they can't or don't want to take it anymore. So the company loses good employees, morale and productivity suffer, the company gets a bad rep, and so on.

Comaford has good suggestions for companies, including rewarding victims and witnesses who speak up, and hooking performance evaluations to company-enhancing behaviors for bullies. They measure up or they are out. As with all things, your own experience must be your guide. If and when you are being bullied, you can try approaching your company and see what happens. And don't feel bad about whatever you decide, whether you decide to leave or look the other way, as long as *you* decide. A lot of people give way to "the great intimidators" rather than have every day ruined by them.[53]

And one more thing . . . be flattered! It's a myth that bullies pick on the weak. Remember, we are all divvying up resources to survive and to thrive, so more than likely you have some tangible or intangible resource that the bully does not. Maybe you are smarter, maybe you have coveted skills or abilities, maybe you are happier, maybe you are better looking, maybe people like you. Who knows? Just know that this is happening because of how amazing you are rather than because you are not. You got this, okay? Here's another common case of sometimes good, sometimes horrid.

Women vs. Women

I'm sorry. It's true. Women do it to women too. At Harvard Medical, I was honored to be selected to become an organizational development trainer. They put us in a train-the-trainers program, with breakout groups. There were four women and one man in my group. They gave us one of those horrible math word problems that you see on the SATs. I was not that good at those, but for some strange reason, this time I had the answer almost immediately. We were competing against other teams, so I was pretty excited, but wanted to behave myself, so I said calmly, "I got it."

No response. So I waited a little bit and then said it again, and then again. At some point, the other women said they couldn't do it. "Let's ask Ted." I said again that I had the answer, but, yeah, all the women just wanted to hear from the man, who did not have the answer. Maybe that wouldn't happen today. And maybe the fact that female economists in a 1993 study rejected female proposals for National Science Foundation funding more often than did the men also wouldn't happen today.[54] Except I know that it does happen, because my clients tell me so. What is the point of it all? See if what comes next, about chimpanzees, helps you to understand. It helps me.

The alpha male chimpanzee shares his meat with other males to help keep him in power, and with his mother and girlfriends to help get his genes into the next generation, and to keep the babies strong so they get into the next and the next. [55] Females compete for the male's meat. And it can be vicious. In *Women Versus Women: The Uncivil Business War,* we get an example of my training group's mentality from earlier times: "From the earliest of times women have put their total faith in those who held power, thus making male dominance a self-fulfilling prophecy. Goddesses were given short shrift when gods commanded. This could not have happened without female acceptance and consent. Perhaps women were jealous of their own goddesses."[56]

I don't know if getting the math problem right makes me a goddess, but this really is too bad. And to make matters worse, it is largely covert because women have always needed each other: "Few women can survive without bonding to at least one or two other women. Women seek female approval as much as they seek male approval. Therefore, most girls and women deny even to themselves that they envy or compete, even indirectly, with those upon whom they also depend."[57]

Here we are right back to *the look*. In this case, *the look of other women*. And we are back to the same approach. You may fight, flee, or submit—and we are going to talk about this more. For now, just make sure that whatever it is you do, *you are the decider*, so you don't get depressed. And please remind yourself to be flattered! If you are the target of this envy, it is because there is something wonderful about you. I know, it hurts. Just don't make it worse. And that applies to bullying, female envy, and workplace sibling rivalry too.

Sibling Rivalry at Work

Sibling rivalry at work? You bet. In the mammalian world, since procreation is the thing, a mother nurses her offspring until it begins to appear that the offspring has become better able to find its own food. At that point, it becomes a better parental investment for her to spend herself and her calories suckling a newer, younger sibling. Since she cannot even make a new baby until she has stopped nursing, at some point mothers wean their young to prepare for bearing a subsequent offspring, even if they do not have one. According to Steven Pinker's *How the Mind Works*, "The young mammal puts up a holy stink, hounding the mother for access to the teat for weeks or months before acquiescing."[58] Bottle-fed babies put up a holy stink too. And this could well be the holy stink you see at work. Bear with me here.

By this account, we all wanted to take more than our parents wanted to give, the implication of which is staggering.

Could it be that somewhere within each and every one of us lives a deep-seated and too-easily triggered experience of having wanted more than we got—that and a keen eye for who else might be getting some or more of whatever it is we want? No matter if you were an only child, you got weaned too, left wanting something you couldn't have because of some other kid who never even materialized. So naturally it's tough to just sit there and watch someone else at work getting more recognition, a better title, better pay, more work-from-home hours, special attention from the alpha male, or the alpha female, or whatever. Not without your feeling at least a twinge of something you wish you didn't feel and more than likely wouldn't tell anyone you did.

You were not asking for that much. All we ever really want is to be the center of the universe forevermore, and when that doesn't happen, we might throw a fit, a fit with legs. Take baboons: "50% of aggression is displacement aggression onto an innocent bystander. A male loses a fight, chases a sub adult male, who bites a juvenile, who chases an adult female, who slaps an infant—and almost everyone feels better afterwards."[59]

Strategic Management

In Ernest Becker's *Denial of Death,* we learn how deeply terrified humans are of dying and how we spend our entire lives trying to deny and prevent the one thing we know is sure to occur.[60] To cope, we can either latch on to power (competing for a special place alongside the parent, the teacher, the boss, etc.) or we can try to become that power (competing for a place above all of the above). Could it be that every time I turned down an opportunity for my own professional advancement, telling myself that it was for the good of my nest, that I was choosing to latch on to power rather than to become it? That would be called a "powerful alliances" strategy.[61]

To find out about your own strategies, you may go to Annette Simmons's book *Territorial Games* for a grid of ten games used by you and used on you by people at work. Like "strategic noncompliance." That one is about people who, for example, like to suggest setting up a task force to study the situation, when it is really their strategy to buy a little time to figure out how to kill yours.

But come on, we are not *all bad*. We love, we cooperate, we care for our kin, we fulfill obligations. We are not strictly competitive. Empathy is a strategy too.[62] Still, everybody is doing something. The politician's (or resource seeker's) "ultimate aim (whether he knows it or not) is status,"[63] because for all those years among our ancestors, status expanded access to the choicest survival goodies: the choicest food, the choicest sex, the choicest shelter. So we can just forget all those high-minded ideas about eliminating hierarchy in organizations. As if no one really cares anymore about titles, compensation, bonus, promotions.

We all need to think we're good, even when we're not, until and unless we get exposed, and then we get defensive. How many of us will admit to ourselves how downright petty and immature we can be? The real beauty of it all is how we manage to keep these aspects of our being, such as status-seeking, all so unconscious that we can just keep on doing what we are doing without feeling ashamed. Handy for the intimidators. By the way, snakes don't have to kill each other to assert dominance over another snake. Top-Snake just has to wrestle the other snake down. Sometimes just assuming one of a number of dominance postures will do the trick. Human snakes don't exactly have to kill either to put people in their place. They can just use *the look* to assert their territorial dominance over everybody else. And what are you supposed to do about that?

Resource-Holding Potential

Here is how you know whether you should fight, flee, submit, or negotiate when things are not going the way you want them to. You calculate your resource-holding potential (RHP), which is a calculation of an animal's capacity to win a fight based on the resources it has going for it.[64] Did you know that dung beetles fight over dung balls, and the one with the biggest ball (resource) gets the girl?[65] Resources can be anything: constituencies, alternative career opportunities, valued expertise. Whatever it is, just calculate the relative resource-holding potential of the parties involved to increase your chances of deciding correctly how to respond. Resource value (V) is what you are willing to invest of yourself for the cause, so don't forget to factor that in too.

There will be an exercise on RHP and V for you to play with at the end of this chapter. But first I want to tell you about "the big don't."

The Big Don't

Whatever you do, do not waste an ounce of your precious energy trying to change anyone else. As one journalist put it, "The best place to start when we have problems with others is the last place we look: the mirror."[66] Fine, go ahead, mention whatever it is that is killing you to the offender once, twice at the most, but then that's it. Otherwise, you risk turning yourself into someone who barely resembles the otherwise classy person you know you are—when you become whining, complaining, controlling, miserable . . . by your own hand. Don't do that. Here's another way.

Case Example

Elizabeth was on the high end of sensitivity to *the look*. Too often, she got triggered emotionally by what she thought people thought about who she was and what she thought and said. The energy drain was adversely affecting her whole life. Elizabeth got **grounded** in the belief that she would, one way or another, find a way to ease this pain for herself, and for the people in her life, and **recognized** that she would have to work on tempering her internal-environment sensitivity for any place she might work or live. Elizabeth began to take things less personally, understanding that everyone else was just trying to get through the day, and up-level their own careers, in the best way they knew how.

As things eased for Elizabeth, she became intensely curious about whether there were external environments that would be easier and friendlier than the one in which she was currently working. So, just for the fun of it, she began to **explore** opportunities on the other side of the country and in other industries too, and took **action** that landed her an offer at a company where she already had friends. It turned out that although things were better, they did not feel better enough. The friends had friends who were too highly competitive and spoiled the well. Elizabeth had dreams about how teams should be. So with her improved confidence and well-being, she calculated her RHP and competed for a higher-level position that would help her to create the world she wants to live in as a leader of these teams.

Elizabeth got the job, and as happy as she is with her success, Elizabeth is **tackling** the inner voice that keeps reminding her that she never did this before. She is responding with the reassurance that she believes she can do this and, if nothing else, wants to know that she tried.

Elizabeth is *Getting to Great in Work and Life* because
Elizabeth learned how to manage her mind. That is what
we are going to talk about next—managing your mind.
And here below is an exercise for you on resource-holding
potential.

Exercise:
Resource-Holding Potential and Value: RHP and V

More than we may know, and now more than ever,
we grapple with whether to fight, flee, or submit—in
our careers, our relationships, with our neighbors.
Resource-holding potential (RHP) is an estimation
of your *ability* to get what you want, based on what
leverage or resources you do or don't have working
for you. Resource value (V) is your *motivation*—
what you are willing to invest of yourself to get from
here to there.

This exercise is designed to help you practice putting
the higher brain in charge of these life-shaping
decisions. Let's use work as an example. Suppose
you are trying to figure out whether to go up against
other internal candidates for a promotion at your
company.

To Practice:

Taking into consideration such factors as relative
rank in the organization, nature of constituencies,
how easily you or the other party could be replaced,
at what cost/benefit to the organization . . .

- Estimate your own RHP and V, respectively, on a scale of 1 to 10.

- On a scale of 1 to 10, repeat the estimations of RHP and V, respectively, for the other candidates.

- Now compare which of you is in the stronger position to win the "fight," and factor this into your decision of what course of action to take.

- Maybe you are inspired to go for it (fight), to negotiate your way forward. Maybe you recognize you need to leave this company to reach this level at another company (flee). Maybe you recognize you need to work on increasing your own RHP before you step up (submit, but not in a bad way—in fact, for the good).

- The numbers will give you something less emotional and more concrete to look at as you examine your options. But bear in mind that a very high or low V (motivation to win) can make all the difference in outcome, when ability is equal or close.

We all care intensely for the narrative of our own life and very much want it to be a good story, with a decent hero.
~ *Daniel Kahneman*

4
MANAGING YOUR MIND

A Decent Hero

"THERE'S SOMETHING ABOUT HER," said the infectious disease doctor to the surgeons who wanted to amputate my upper right quadrant. I never did find out what exactly is included in the upper right quadrant. It seemed to me there would be something in there you might need. Not my area of expertise, but I was smart enough to figure out that it was a whole lot more than just my breast and my arm. This was the big one. The bad one. Necrotizing fasciitis, a.k.a. *flesh-eating disease*. It was the same strep A as strep throat, only it is deadly in your arm.

One by one, too many grim-faced doctors stopped by my hospital stretcher in the hallway to tell me that I had a 95 percent chance of dying—that they would have to take my arm (short for "upper right quadrant") to save my life. It is a long and pretty crazy story that involved three attempts to get into the hospital, seven weeks in the hospital, ten trips to the OR for debriding and skin grafting from my leg to my arm, four months out of work, then another four months of disabled employment after that, with six months of daily trips to OT post–hospital discharge. All I did every day was meet each need that was before me in the best way I knew how. And when the angel of death, the infectious disease doctor, asked, "How stoic are you?" I said simply, "I'm not stoic; I'm busy." Now, ask me how I felt then and I will tell you this: *I felt strong and proud.*

The telling of the story here leaves out way, way more than I am including. The point here is that after years of misplaced dependency, this time I was going to take care of myself in this most heroic and "pleasant" way. That's how the medical record described my demeanor in the ER, while they were ignoring me, and sending me home repeatedly misdiagnosed. "Pleasant." And I would add I was a decent but not perfect "hero" because as good as I was, I was also completely out of touch with the real need that was before me in the most critical moment of my life.

In retrospect, I am convinced that the "something" about me that saved my upper right quadrant—and my life—had everything to do with my meditation practice and the more mindful way that I had learned to live in the world. I was steady and strong with light in my eyes. They thought I could fight it and I did. So they let me keep my arm. On the other hand, to have allowed myself to be turned away from the critical care that I needed not once, but twice? That it could have mattered one whit how my behavior looked to them or to me was very likely part of why I nearly died. I could have thrown a fit and refused to leave, but that would have looked bad. *OMG, the look!* We talked about that.

So let's just say that at the onset of that illness, I was

onto something that I had not yet mastered because true mastery is about this:

> To know when to act and when to refrain from action,
> what is right action and what is wrong.
> (*Bhagavad Gita* 18:30)[67]

True mastery is about meeting the need that is before us in the course of daily living, in the most skillful way possible, even if—and especially if—that means having to let go of some preferred or idealized way of thinking about ourselves.

Bumper Cars

Going back to Ernest Becker's Pulitzer Prize–winning *Denial of Death,* we all spend our lives trying to prevent the one thing that is sure to occur—death. This terrifies us all, whether we know it or not. The "meaning and purpose" we seek in life is good in and of itself, but it is also a way to reassure ourselves that we matter(ed), and are therefore saved from never having existed at all. In Becker's words, we subscribe to "a mythical hero system in which people serve in order to earn a feeling of primary value, or cosmic specialness, of ultimate usefulness to creation, of unshakeable meaning."[68]

The mythical hero system is a story, and we all have a story. As before, the brain can only process so many bits of information, so we have to piece things together into a story that is coherent and acceptable enough to convince us that we matter enough to exist. So there it is. Everyone is scurrying around trying to be the hero of a story they made up, bumping into other people who also have a story in which they are not second place either. Picture that. That's why I call it bumper cars. But on some level we all know that we are mere specks in this vast universe of ours, which is likely what all the pressure and urgency to *spin it* so other people will *buy it* is driven by. This is where developing emotional intelligence (EQ) becomes important, so we can behave intelligently when people have ideas of their own that don't exactly match ours. Often, as you know, people react—unskillfully, as the Dali Lama would say—rather than respond.

Alas, there are times when our storytelling skills are simply no match for the skills of the other. We might speculate that some people are so skilled at spinning their stories that they are able to rise to positions of power over others without having fully developed the other qualities that would keep that power well directed in the interests of all. It is not their fault exactly. Somewhere along the line, by nature, nurture, or both, something happened to them to make their need to secure their own sense of importance a full-time job. But it appears that there may be even more internal/external-environmental interaction than that going on. *The Atlantic* published an article called "Power Causes Brain Damage."[69] Here they found that "the powerful" tended to have damage to the area of the brain associated with the very sensitivity to needs and interests of others that may have contributed to their rise.

This finding is consistent with other findings that both college fraternity presidents and alpha vervet monkeys show hormonal and behavioral changes during their reign. It is as if they are intoxicated by a drug, serotonin.[70] Serotonin is known as the *leadership hormone* because of the high confidence, self-esteem, and relatively low stress that comes along with it. Too much, though, can be associated with avoidance and withdrawal, and a preoccupation with planning that can remove leaders from the people with whom they bonded to get where they are. As one CEO said to his wife, "Everyone is kissing my ring; I have never felt more isolated in my life. I don't feel connected to anyone, and that includes you." If only he had known that it was likely his alpha hormones to blame, he might not have torn his whole family apart, convinced that it was the wife.

Not everyone externalizes like this. At the other end of the spectrum we have the ones who blame and torment themselves.

The Inner Critic

Until just recently, I would not use the term *inner critic*. It seemed so overused. But lately *the inner critic is* alive and kicking for so many people that I decided to take it on. You may want to take a look at *Internal Family Systems Therapy,* by Richard Schwartz and Martha Sweeney, to learn more about the inner critic.[71] Here's my own take. *The inner critic* (we'll call it *TIC*) is a piece of your mind that tells you that no matter how well you do, it is not good enough. In that way it makes you want to do better, until and unless you finally give up under the constant barrage. Still, a lot of people say it spurred them on and got them where they are today.

TIC sees danger, failure, and potential for humiliation everywhere. So it also protects you from making a complete fool, or failure, out of yourself. If it happens to spur us on and keep us out of harm's way, why would we want to give that up—if we even could, which we can't because this negativity bias that has helped us to survive and to thrive is hardwired in.

Left to its own devices, TIC can become so loud in your life that you begin to trust this figment of your imagination more than you trust yourself. Or worse, you get to where you don't even know the difference between its voice and your own. This is how and when the suffering really sets in. And it is bad. TIC's voice may have originated outside of you. Maybe it was an overbearing parent who meant well but overshot. Too much of a good thing, we could say. Or maybe a teacher. But now it is in you, and yours to have and to hold forevermore. If it's in charge of you, instead of the other way around, it can fill you with shame—the very thing it meant to prevent. And shame-filled people tend not to grow. More often it keeps you safe and stuck. So, what can you do?

For one thing, know this: You are not *the inner critic*. You are separate entities. As with marriage, friendship, and work relations, the first step is to recognize and respect how separate we are (or should be). Then there are a number of approaches.

- Some would say to go back and explore how that voice got there in the first place.

- Others would say don't do that; just take what it says and think the opposite. Fake it 'til you make the opposite your own.

- Other approaches include finding an overriding purpose that distracts you from *TIC*.

- Or reframe your story with affirmations about how amazing you are. Take that, *TIC*.

But what we resist persists—big time—so I'm saying let's make friends with it instead. You and *TIC*. And then figure out together the best ways to proceed. This means that when *TIC* gets anxious about how things may unfold, you listen and learn, problem-solve, and reassure *TIC* that you've got this if you do, or factor in what *TIC* has to say if you realize *TIC* actually has a good point. Above all, be respectful; you can deplete yourself down to the bone by fighting with *TIC* all day and all night long. Better to make friends and work it out instead. Here again, we need the higher, adult brain in charge. For this, you need to know how to *manage your mind*.

Managing Your Mind

What if we took control of our breath? This is like rebooting your computer when it gets all messed up. It's twitching. It freezes. Too many programs open; all the wires are crossed. What do the techs tell you to do? Shut down and reboot. The same goes for you. Thinking, thinking, thinking yourself into a deep, dark hole? Talking, talking, talking yourself into a craze? People around you have had it with you? Reboot yourself. Take hold of yourself—before someone else does.

Usually, when we don't like how things are going, we try to change the other person, place, or thing outside of ourselves. Have you ever tried to go on a diet, to start exercising, to stop smoking, to keep your mouth shut, to call your mother more? You know how hard it is to change anything about yourself, even if you want to. So what possesses us to think we can change someone else—who doesn't even want to change? If only that jerk down the hall would . . . Doesn't matter. What a joy, what a relief, *finally*, to be able to make more of a difference than you might ever have imagined simply by taking care of, or charge of, your very own mind. To do this, we just need to know a few simple things about how the mind works.

For one thing, *thoughts are not facts*. For example, in

my signature workshop, "For Busy People: Managing Your MIND—Strategies for a Happier, Healthier, Productive Life," I ask people to close their eyes and imagine that a coworker asks, "Hey, what did you think about that memo for the meeting next week?" What meeting? What memo? They didn't get any memo. Then I ask them to tell me quick without overthinking, right from the gut, why they think they didn't see that memo.

Then we capture the individual responses. Boom. Boom. Boom. Responses typically range from "My boss is an idiot" to "I'm so unorganized; it could have been there and I never saw it." Things do seem to split along "blame on them" vs. "shame on me" lines, with most falling in one category or another. What counts here is that given the exact same stimulus (my scenario and instructions), people come up with different responses, different thoughts to explain the situation. This is all the proof we need to know that thoughts are not facts. They are a mix of what actually happened and what the mind makes of what happened, depending on who you are, what you came in with that day, and what you have been through in this play or tragicomedy that we call *LIFE*. So, again, we make up stories, and we really need distance and awareness to get a grip on that. This is where mindfulness comes into play.

Mindfulness

Molecular biologist Jon Kabat-Zinn, widely regarded as the father of Western mindfulness, defined mindfulness as "paying attention in a particular way: on purpose, in the present moment, and nonjudgmentally."[72] An early Davidson, Kabat-Zinn et al. study found that participants in the group who had already received the eight-week mindfulness-meditation training showed more robust immune systems, antibody titers, and responses to flu vaccine as well. Since then, another study by Antoine Lutz et al. found that the kind of compassion that would benefit so many relationships can be taught, a finding supported by brain-circuitry changes showing up on brain scans subsequent to compassion-meditation training.[73]

Mental training has been found to increase attentional acuity and to promote positive emotional experience.[74] Moreover, the relaxation response (RR) in particular has been found to alter gene expression in a way that counters stress.[75] It should also be noted that meditation may have different effects for different people with different struggles.[76] Accordingly, as with any self-help endeavor, please bring your physician in on it with you as you monitor impact along your own way. That said, meditation appears to be especially good exercise for the part of your brain in charge of your attention.[77] Studies on the beneficial effects of meditation are now too numerous to count. And even the studies on power brain damage and hormonal changes suggest that things can be reversed.

Could it be that meditation is just what the doctor ordered to restore your energy at whatever is the low point of your day? And not only restore your energy but jack it up to gamma![78]

Two things here: 1) Gamma is the higher mental activity, the stuff we pride ourselves on; and 2) You don't have to be a Buddhist monk to get to gamma. Even the novices in the Lutz study who trained in compassion meditation for only a week showed an increase in gamma activity, just not as grand. Moreover, you may be able to stay sharper longer, since meditation has been found to offset the cortical thinning associated with age.[79] Cool. But don't take my word for it. Only your own experience can tell you what is true for you.

So, let's get going on some experience for you. Ready to breathe?

Power Breathing

There are many good apps online—e.g., Headspace, and Calm—to teach you how to meditate. Since I study, teach, and practice meditation myself, you can also find an instruction sheet called "The Breathing Room" at madelaineweiss.com. But polyvagal breathing—or power breathing, as I like to call it—is so user friendly as an anywhere, anytime, very quick tool for you that I decided to include it both on my website and here. Power breathing stimulates the parasympathetic nervous system's relaxation response. It has been found to lower stress, build physical and psychological resilience, and improve cognitive function.[80] As in, it calms the system and puts the higher brain in charge. So, to recap this chapter, whether it's to . . .

- advocate your way into the hospital when you are dying (god forbid; I hope that never happens to you),

- negotiate with the inner critic (TIC) in your head,

- exercise emotional intelligence to deal with your board, your boss, your peers, your reports, your spouse, your kids, or your neighbors,

- or make important decisions about your work and your life,

. . . you need the higher brain in charge. Hindu mythology has it that the mind is like a mad monkey jumping up and down, bouncing off the walls. One of my philosophy tutors said that the mind is like a two-year-old who's whining and wreaking havoc all over your entire household. Just as a two-year-old needs care and discipline to survive and to thrive, to be happy and healthy, so too does the mind. We take care of our kids, we take care of our pets, we take care of our cars, our homes, our plants, our teeth, our friends. But how many minutes out of your day do you spend taking care of your mind? And when we think about the impact of the mind on our whole entire life, and the lives of everyone we touch, how can we not give it the care and attention it deserves?

Oh, how I wish the ER physician who refused me antibiotics and pain medication, and who kept sending me home when I was so sick and pleading to be admitted, had spent a little more time refining his mind. Naturally, I therefore found it such a privilege to routinely address the medical students, when I was at Harvard, at the beginning and the end of their first-year anatomy course. These students would one day touch the lives of so many, some with empathy, some not, and here was a chance for me to help. What a window of opportunity, when they were about to stand with reverence before their cadavers, for them to practice staying in touch with their own full-blown humanity without becoming so overwhelmed by it that they cut off their emotions and shut down. That's what people do when it's all too much; they simply shut down. Like David.

Case Example

It's not that David lives a small life. He travels internationally for work he enjoys and lives with a woman he loves. David is soft spoken and intelligent, with a racing mind that drives him nuts. It did not take much to get David **grounded** in the belief that things could be different. Things had to be different since he felt overwhelmed and paralyzed by the thoughts in his head and could not stand living like that. And since he did not want to be dependent on medication, he **recognized** that making a difference in his life would have to begin with his own mind. So, in our first session, I taught David *power breathing*. And when he was finished, all he said was "Wow." Other people finish up and say, "Nice." But he was blown away by how very different and how much better he felt in only three breaths.

Left to its own devices, the normal human mind wanders 70 percent of the time.[81] An earlier large-scale study found that the mind was, in general, unhappier when it was wandering than when it was not.[82] But not always. Professor Gabriele Oettingen's research has found that people who envision their wants and wishes are less likely to attain them if the envisioning itself is so satisfying that no action takes place to actually make the dream come true.[83] Sure, there are benefits to mind-wandering—e.g., planning, problem-solving, creativity—but sometimes too much of that good thing can scramble things up or slow things down so bad that nothing gets done.

David had big life decisions to make, the kind that should be made with a clear, calm, and focused higher brain in charge. Once David had the hang of how to kick things upstairs in this way, he was able to begin **exploring** the many wonderful opportunities before him, e.g., graduate school, advancement on the job, or taking a time-out to work on the upcoming political campaign. His **action** was to pause the pursuit of his well-being until midsummer when he would resurrect his exploration of which alternative would be the best internal/external-environmental fit for him going forward. If we learned anything from Covid-19, it is that deliberate pausing is an action too, sometimes the most useful and important one of all. David is back now and happily moving forward and **tackling** his tendency to obsess when it is time to decide as he is *Getting to Great in Work and Life.*

Exercise:
Power Breathing

In our modern world and way of living, cognitive processes—such as attention, memory, planning, reasoning, problem-solving—are essential to our well-being and success. "Stressed-out" breathing throws the breather into fight-or-flight mode. In this state, the higher brain functions are secondary to more primitive, fight-or-flight, lower brain processes.

Power breathing, which fills the belly instead of the chest with air, is an especially good reset to bring clear, calm higher brain functioning back online for better work, play, love, and life.

To Practice:

- You may close your eyes or simply gaze downward.

- Now, begin to breathe. Long, slow, luxurious breaths.

- In through the nose. Out through the nose.

- Belly out on the in-breath. Belly in on the out-breathe.

- Practice a minimum of three power breaths each time, working up to several times a day, until it becomes easy, natural, and at your disposal anywhere, anytime—to calm you and put your higher brain in charge.

Better than if there were thousands of meaningless words
is one meaningful word that on hearing brings peace.

~ Dhammapada

5

MASTERING YOUR MOUTH

To Speak or Not to Speak?

SOMETIMES WE SHOULD HOLD OUR TONGUES—like
when we know that we are provoking someone we love, in
my case my father, and that the odds are good there will be
hell to pay for mouthing off again. Keep on doing what you
are doing, and you keep on getting what you get, or worse.
Then there are times when we should have spoken up but
didn't, like in the hospital ER, when I needed to advocate
for my life. There are times when we are "talking" without
even talking at all, as with Grandmom Rose—some of the
best conversations ever, without a single spoken word. And
there are times when the conversation starts out with no
words and finishes up in words years later than it should
have. Here is an example of that.

Not too long ago I attended a meeting of around twenty
people, mostly women. At some point, the women started

talking about how hard it is to get ahead because the men hog all the air in the room and they, the women, don't even get a chance to talk. Everybody nodded, yeah, yeah, at which point I asked if I could tell a little story, as follows:

I love lamb chops. So does my brother. When we were growing up my mother would make them once a week, and I would sit there and watch my brother eat them all. One day, only about six months ago, my brother, out of the blue in no particular context, said to me, "I was always so happy that you didn't like lamb chops; more for me." My point to the women was that if no one even knew I loved lamb chops because I never said a word about it, who is that on? My brother or me?

And you may be wondering, because I am, how I could confront my father so much, mostly about the ladies' wear that he made in his factory and insisted I wear, but did not confront my brother about the lamb chops. I can only guess that I must have cared more about what I wore (*the look*?) than what I ate. In any case, this chapter on *mastering your mouth* is about talking, not eating.

Let's start with Eastern philosophy. Eastern philosophy espouses concepts such as measured speech, austerity of speech, right speech—basically, the idea that speech should be true, kind, beneficial, and necessary. Whenever I give a workshop and introduce this concept of right speech, people start scribbling frantically on their notepads as if they just heard something really important that they never heard before. Well, they are right; it is important. So why haven't they heard it before? We need it just as much as the people in the East do, maybe more. What's in the way? Maybe it would help if we took a look at why we talk at all. Let's do that.

The First Talker

The first talker could have been *Homo habilis,* two million years ago, and/or *Homo erectus,* one million years ago, or it could have been neither one of them but maybe *Homo sapien* only 200,000 years ago instead.[84] For those of you who want to dig in deeper here, you may help yourselves to the article "Cortical Memory Mechanisms and Language Origins"[85] where you will find no less than 200 references talking to you about talking. Another study lets us know that people generally "talk at a rate of two to four words per second and make an error every 1,000 words or so."[86]

Interesting, but here's what matters for our purposes: To be sure, talking is a social plus, and one that has helped us to survive and to thrive all along, maybe for millions of years if those who believe that talking may have coincided with hunting—and those who think *Homo habilis* the toolmaker was a hunter—are right. How else could our ancestors negotiate who got to eat how much and which cut of the meat from the hunt? How else would they have been able to make deals, detect cheaters, alert each other to danger, and the like? Why couldn't they just do it with the wave of a hand or a point of the finger—"Berries over here, ferocious beast over there"? Because finger-pointing wouldn't work in the dark, for one thing, and even if it was light out, they'd have to be looking at each other all the time, just in case someone decided to "say" something with their finger—instead of either resting their eyes or using them to scan outward for food, danger, sex opportunities, and the like.

Something else was needed, so evolution came up with the idea of using the human tongue for communication:

> While virtually every other muscle group in the body engaged in a vital activity fairly regularly, the tongue

just sort of lay in the mouth between meals, doing little except help with swallowing saliva. The brain, like a patient Olympics coach, taught the tongue to perform a wide range of acrobatic gymnastics. . . . [T]he langue (tongue) in language became the indispensable shaper of speech.[87]

By putting the tongue to work, hands could do all kinds of useful things, like carrying babies, tools, and other objects, so our early ancestors could move more easily to safer environments, where more food and water could be found.

Mouth noise was magic. Make the noise, and dreams come true. A baby cries, and food comes, clean diaper, a warm blanket, just about whatever it wants. *And, oh, that look on her face and the sound of her voice; here she comes, and she loves me. I'm all set.* Psyching out the thoughts and intentions of other people is emotional intelligence. This is how we know what people do and don't want to hear come out of our mouths, how we keep from getting fired or slapped at work. We are mind readers. From the get-go. They don't teach it in school. They don't have to. Even monkeys who don't go to school have "mirror neurons" that fire both when the monkey is doing a task and when the monkey is observing another doing the same task.

This suggests to scientists that the brain is set up to connect with the physical and mental states of others through our experience of our own: "For language to evolve, humans needed a viable theory about the minds of other people—otherwise they'd just be talking to themselves."[88] So, with our mind-reading abilities to guide us, from crying to cooing to babbling to a few simple words by the end of the first year, little by little we learn to use this tool that is our tongue (and jaw and lips and teeth and hard and soft palates, uvula, larynx, lungs), until someday we are able to make it all work in the most amazing life- and culture-shaping ways. For better and for worse.

Leader Talk

Language is both a uniter and a divider. Even within the same nation or tribal affiliation, dialects develop which strengthen in-group loyalty and out-group discrimination. Class distinctions, age-group differences, subcultural affiliations (e.g., professional identities, such as doctors, lawyers, soldiers, oil rig operatives) are all served by the use of special accents, terminologies, acronyms, and tones of voice.[89]

Language conveys status and intimacy. If the corporate culture uses profanity, you're in if you do too, and not if you don't. There is language to fit in, but there is also language to stand out. Maybe you take this as a given and have never even asked why, but language researchers have theories about why people take turns trying to say brilliant things at meetings. These public displays of oratorical brilliance are known among language researchers as "relevance displays."[90]

Probably you have seen it yourself, speakers making outright fools of themselves trying to make interesting, relevant points for leadership status. They talk so people will listen, or at least they try, and sometimes do well. Leadership done well is a good thing. It is a central organizing feature of group life, no matter what size. In fact, I learned and observed in business school that because leadership abhors a vacuum, people can't get much done until and unless the "who is in charge" and "who is in good with who is in charge" questions get resolved.

The purpose of leadership through the ages was not just to make one person feel good about him/herself, but really to keep it all running smoothly for everyone. After all, at the very least, someone had to make and communicate decisions about who did what work and who got what reward. And someone had to settle the inevitable disputes over who did what work and who got what reward. So, to our question, to speak or not to speak: if all of that is a responsibility you want, and you really do have something interesting and important to say, know that displays of interesting and important language can help get you that job—making it a good time to speak.

Peer Talk

Language is, of course, critically important peer-to-peer too. Group sizes got bigger and bigger as we moved from berry-picking to hunting to farming societies. Language evolved as a way to help us share what we know that might help others, to let others know what we need for ourselves and our kin, to alert each other to danger, and to make sure that the rules for relatively peaceful coexistence are clear. As populations grew in number and complexity, we wouldn't have wanted then, nor do we want now, for every bit of that people stuff in the internal environment to wind up on leadership's plate. So language gave us a way to do some of our own business with each other, words we can say to influence each other in the direction we hope things will go, for the public good as well as our own. Public esteem and persuasion matter if you want to get ahead and get along; so do chitchat and gossip.

Chitchat and Gossip

Chitchat is a kind of verbal exchange that is not particularly suffused with meaning and purpose. But it doesn't always have to be. Sometimes it is simply the sound of our voice that is needed, as with lemurs, who reaffirm social bonds with their kin when far away, through the sound of their voice. Another example of verbal exchange that passes for something other than what it may really be is gossip.

People gossip. You might have done it once or twice yourself, as do chimps. Grooming is an exchange of socially important information. Who grooms whom is how chimps know who can be trusted, who's on top, who's in, and who's out. If you are out, you don't get fed, so it matters to know where you stand with whom. One study found that over 50 percent of workplace conversation is gossip.[91] And there is something called prosocial gossip that helps to keep evildoers in check.[92] But even if you or they have the best of intentions, gossip can be a serious trust buster and have the opposite effect. So can lying.

Lying

Lying is just like gossip. Researcher Tim Levine found that 87 percent of lying is either to socially promote or protect the one doing the lying, or to otherwise ingratiate the lying one to others.[93] As we discussed, looking good matters because, back in the day, if people didn't think well of us, we might not get fed. Reputation matters if we want to survive and to thrive in today's world of work too, as much as ever before. Lying is a normal, natural, and good part of child development.[94] Key words: *child* and *development*-- as in, we are supposed to outgrow it. Unfortunately, a lot of people don't, but kids who do go on to do better in life as adults. As Harvard ethicist and prominent thinker on the subject Sissela Bok said in her book *Lying: Moral Choice in Public and Private Life*, "Whatever matters to human beings, trust is the atmosphere in which it thrives."[95]

Most adults feel anxious when they lie. Except the more we do it, the easier it gets, and, therefore, the more we do it. Researchers have found that the brain's amygdala is responsible for the sickening pain of fear, guilt, and anxiety we feel when we lie, a measurable experience that brain scans have shown to diminish with each passing lie.[96] It's as if the brain allowing the lying has been calmed, reassured— if not inspired—that it lied and lived to lie another day. Phew. It's all good, says the brain. But it's not. Lying can cause brain damage and ruin reputations. If it is hard to control, try to find help, or try another way to matter that might yield a better internal and external result. What about negotiating your way forward instead?

Negotiating

From psychologist Leigh Thompson: Negotiating is an "interpersonal decision-making process" that is "necessary whenever we cannot achieve our objectives single-handedly."[97] I find this definition respectful, honest, and useful in its recognition that negotiation is not always our first-choice way to get things done. On the other hand, remember what we said about the bumper cars, i.e., how everyone has a story about how things should be that we are all trying to get other people to buy into. In that sense, we are negotiating or "interpersonal decision-making" virtually all of the time. Awake or asleep; check out your dreams.

The bigger and more complex our external environment became, the bigger and more complex our internal environment, the human social brain, became in dealing with it all. Good thing to know. So, when to speak? Do not speak while the other person is talking. We all have to get our story out, so we have to take turns, something else we have been doing since the beginning of our time. Of course, that doesn't mean we're always listening the way we should be: "The speed of response (about 200 milliseconds on average, about the same time as it takes to blink) is astonishing when we appreciate the slow nature of language encoding: it takes 600ms to prepare a word for delivery. This implies a substantial overlap between listening to the current speaker and preparing our own response."[98]

Yikes. But you knew that, right? You could feel it, in them and in you. It's not our fault. Nature makes us do what once helped us to survive and to thrive. Except we don't need to respond quite that quickly anymore. Nothing is going to eat us if we don't, so let's just power breathe, take a pause, and when the other person is finished talking, repeat back what you heard.

I had to practice this repeating back when I was in negotiation and mediation training, and resisted mightily due to how incredibly awkward and unnatural it felt. I did not know then what I just told you about those milliseconds hardwired into our brains, and that explains a lot. And I have to say that in the role plays, when someone repeated back to me what I had said, I practically fell in love, or at least felt more motivated to meet the other person halfway than I felt before the repeating back occurred. Repeating back is such a good example of "when to speak" that I highly recommend you practice this with everyone you know, at work, at home, and wherever you may roam. Even so, there can be communication snafus. Humans have something for that too.

Repairing

Humans are also hardwired to repair their communications when they misfire. In fact, scientists have found that we repair communications every ninety seconds, across cultures and languages, by saying things like "huh," or some other form of asking for further clarification.[99] This fits very nicely with repeating back, so calling for clarification is also a good "when to speak" moment, as long as we ask for clarification in a way that does not rudely interrupt. And that we are wired for repairing also emphasizes how hard human communications can be, as I imagine you know.

I happen to think that talking is altogether overrated as a cure-all for everything that ails us, within and between us. For example, talking over and over again about one's trauma at some point only strengthens the neural connections associated with the trauma, keeping the trauma alive and firing over and over again, rather than easing the strength of it for us. At home and at work, going over the trouble again and again can do the same thing in the same way to make things not better but worse. And then there are the conversations we have with TIC, the inner critic, inside of our heads; many of those are beyond useless by now.

If we are trying to express ourselves into existence, to shore up social bonds, to share knowledge and move things along in constructive ways, to meet our needs to thrive and grow for the good of ourselves and others (that is what we are trying to do, right?), when talk that aims to be true, kind, necessary, and beneficial isn't helping, what can we do instead?

Alternatives to Talking

WRITING: Yes, we can write. Writing instead of talking. On the writing alternative, one study found a positive relation between writing and both physical and emotional health, as long as you are doing something more constructive than just writing your negative thoughts over and over again.[100] Careful about this venting idea. As with trauma, the repetition can just lock it in and make it worse. Short of that, it can help. Blessed be our hands. Given how I almost lost one, I know I love mine.

DANCING: The unity of dancing is programmed into us genetically as the message "we are part of the same team; we are on the same side; we are all one."[101] Bees do it too—wriggle together. So the next time you are going round and round and getting nowhere with someone, inside or outside of your head, why not dance instead? Or sing?

SINGING: Studies of people with Alzheimer's and Parkinson's found that "singing sessions appeared to have positive effects on participants' cognitive powers, their physical ability and their emotions."[102] Singing is good. As long as it doesn't put an "earworm" into your partner's or office mate's head and they can't get it out.[103] Otherwise it's good as an alternative to talking when talking is doing no good. As we have said before, mastery—in this case mastery of your mouth—is "*to* know when to act and when to refrain from action, what is right action and what is wrong."[104]

Sometimes it is true, kind, necessary, and beneficial to talk. And sometimes other things are better options, including but not limited to just being still. You will figure it out for yourself. Talking, writing, dancing, singing, nothing . . . Choose and choose well—with your higher brain in charge. Here below is a case example of *mastering your mouth*, and an exercise to follow.

Case Example

Victor is a high-powered business executive with a successful career, a wife who adores him, and an external environment with more friction and stress at work and home than he felt he could bear. Because Victor grew up in chaos, it was not surprising that he married a woman who would contribute control to their life together—too much control. *Grounding* in the belief that things could be different and better was a direct result of Victor's experimentation with power breathing because, through power breathing, Victor noticed that things were already different and better. Victor also **recognized** that the best leverage for improving his home situation would be with his internal responses, over which he could gain better control.

Victor began to **explore** his triggers, and to differentiate between where he would hold the line and where he could give way. After all, his wife had a career with hefty responsibility of her own, and was suffering from the friction too. Victor decided to experiment with something small enough that it would not overwhelm them, and big enough that it would get them on their way. So, for example, in the past, he would bicker with his wife over her telling him how to bag the trash. He worried that keeping it inside would put a wedge between them, make him sick, or mess up things at work when he displaced his anger there. The **action** he took was to tell his wife that although he was fine with how he bagged the trash, he could see this meant a lot to her, and because he loves her, he would bag the trash the way she prefers.

His wife was touched enough by his overture to say that it really didn't matter, that she was fine with how he bagged the trash. She acknowledged, to herself and to him, that she really just needs him to take the time to show her and tell her that she matters too, that she is appreciated and loved. For Victor, whose job is so stressful and family responsibilities with his parents and siblings so steep, it was always easier to just hold it all in until he erupted with careless and hurtful words and then keep on doing the thing she didn't like, all of which damaged the very relationship most supportive of him.

Their next step was to apply the new way of being together to their issues with money. Until this more artful use of words becomes the new automatic—at work, at home, and with his parents and siblings—Victor is, with good success, **tackling** his habit of holding it in and then carelessly blurting it out. Victor and his wife have become good company for each other as they are *Getting to Great in Work and Life.*

Exercise:
Mastering Your Mouth

Shakespeare said, "There is nothing either good or bad, but thinking makes it so." Does it ever! The mind loves categories, and well it should. For one thing, category-making is how we know the difference between what we can eat and what can eat us. But sometimes the mind makes mistakes (turns out it is only a rope, not really a snake). And too often we have acted from the mouth on our mistake.

This exercise is intended to bring discipline over the mind's potential to make snap (and sometimes silly) judgments, to sharpen awareness of reality, and improve our mastery over the mouth with regard to it.

To Practice:

- Sit comfortably in your seat, with your eyes open to the world around you (e.g., looking out a window).

- Suspend categorizing by simply observing whatever is before you.

- Every time you find yourself thinking ABOUT what you are seeing (trees, cars, smokestacks, clouds, tables, chairs), return to just seeing. This is hard.

- It helps to practice "just being" with experience because it is difficult to separate the raw experience from our judgments about them. Once we can "just be" with experience, we no longer have to shoot from the mouth about what is right and wrong with everyone else.

- We can pause, repeat back what we have heard, and ask for clarification, all of which can make things better than they might otherwise be.

- You may do this with hearing instead of seeing, e.g., every time you find yourself thinking ABOUT what you are hearing.

- Holding oneself to this exercise for at least three to five minutes is recommended.

PART II:
GETTING TO GREAT IN LIFE

No road is long
with good company.
~ Turkish Proverb

6

WORK-LIFE QUALITY

Good Company

I ONCE ATTENDED a weeklong philosophy exercise at a most magnificent compound. Everything was gorgeous: the grounds, the lake, the marble interiors, the people, the teachings, the flowers and the organic vegetarian food, arranged like artwork in bursts of color that made me gasp the first time I entered the dining room. Their profound love of beauty in all things—their very insistence on it—seemed foreign to me. I thought beauty was something you either did or didn't have, and if you did, well, then people might resent you for it. All of a sudden, beauty became a universal virtue and necessity in a way that I never experienced before. So was *service*.

When we were not performing service—gardening, cooking, loading/unloading a commercial-sized dishwasher in a steam-filled room, rolling up the massive oriental rugs, taking them off the porch, shaking them out, then

rolling them up again and putting them back onto the
porch—we were singing Baroque in round (mortifying),
and reading Shakespeare, the Upanishads, and transcripts
of conversations between the school's founder and the
spiritual leaders of that time. This week was filled with some
of the hardest work that I have ever done . . . and some of
the most brilliant, big-hearted, and funny doctors, lawyers,
nurses, teachers, social workers, information technologists,
physicists, economists, and just plain good company I had
ever met. That's why, after shopping around a bit, I settled
on this group to become my new intellectual family.

There were eggheads in my life as I was growing up—
eggheads who kept me good company when I visited with
them every Friday night (while the whole rest of the world
was out playing with their friends). These were Grandmom
Rose's clan, which explains my regular meetings with her
picture on top of the TV set. Uncles Sidney and Rudy,
Aunts Adele, Sarah, and Ev; these funny people who read
books and did crossword puzzles. All dead now. And after
the retreat, here I found this whole group of smart, funny
people who were not dead and on top of my TV set—a whole
group of people from around the world mixing it up on
philosophy with the rest of the students and me.

One of the many precious contributions they made to
my life was the concept of *good company*. There is a whole
book by the same name that explains it all, a book they
brought to my bedside in the hospital when they all thought
I was going to die.[105] Good company has to do with quality,
not quantity, so I'm guessing they wanted me to have a
quality death, which is fine. For the living, however, good
company is the highest quality we can find and afford of
the food we eat, the wine we drink, the books we read, the
music we listen to, the company we keep, and the company

that we are to ourselves—all to nourish the heart, mind, body, and soul.

And now you know why I say work-life *quality* instead of work-life *balance*. Balance sounds too much like it implies equal allocations of time for this part of life and that, which I do not believe is the best way to nourish one's being. Okay then, what is? Seems to me the best way to tend our lives is with attention to a blend of what matters most and what we can do something about. Happiness researcher Sonja Lyubomirsky found that 50 percent of the happiness differences among us are genetically set, i.e., based on our internal environment. Even more important, I think, is that only 10 percent is associated with life circumstances like marital status and income, or external-environment stressors we confront.[106]

This means that we can quit agonizing over that person or policy we can't do anything about because a whopping 40 percent of our happiness (or unhappiness) is associated with something else. Lyubomirsky's research suggests that the 40 percent is associated with intentional activity, daily behavioral choices, and the mindset driving these choices— what we do and how we think, and stuff we can actually do something about. It seems that to be happiest we should focus our attention on what we can control in the key areas of our lives that matter to us most.

Great. Which areas are those? There is an exercise at the end of this chapter to help you figure that out. For now, however, one area of our lives that I would like to put a line under is the physical environment in which we work and live. Research suggests physical environment really does impact our lives, and it is something we can do something about.

No Place Like Home
If a great life depends on a great fit between humans and

the environments in which they work and live, then this has
to include not just the people in our external environments
but also the physical environments themselves. People who
study environmental psychology believe that we humans
long for our ancestral home. They talk about our enjoyment
of landscape art, and of our own lawns and gardens, as
manifestations of this yearning. This idea also helps to
explain why when I was given a very small, renovated office
that had been a broom closet before I got there, the first
thing I did was put up a picture of a garden with a little
bench that I could imagine sitting on. Our longing for the
lush openness of our ancestral environment may also be
why "nature" is considered to be such a good stress buster
and blood pressure reducer for us.[107]

At some point, however—researchers believe around
400,000 years ago—hominins (modern humans and our
immediate ancestors) were enjoying semipermanent,
more-indoor versions of "home."[108] Since we had by then
taken control of fire, we were able to ward off dangerous
animals so we could sleep and eat together in a single space.
From there we began to use closed-in spaces for more than
just shelter. As communities grew larger, communal spaces
were built for toolmaking, and so people could congregate,
not just to make decisions affecting them all, but also to
share stories and catch up on the news of the day. Fast-
forward to today, and we have bleak and barren concrete
spaces where people convene, when we can, for all of these
same things. This should matter to us more than we let
it, because there actually are benefits to correcting the
mismatch between who we are and how we live.

Research shows that we can decrease the environmental
mismatch and, in so doing, increase the health, well-being,
job satisfaction, and productivity of employees, as well as

the company's bottom line.[109] A number of savanna-like steps include sunlight, greenery, and places and policies to support napping, exercise, and social interaction too. As it stands, too many of our work spaces are grossly mismatched with our human nature. And although at the time of Covid it was not clear how many of our workers would even be returning to these work spaces, it was clear that many wished they could continue to work from home. But there are problems there too.

Houses are getting bigger and bigger without making the people living in them any happier.[110] If the ego made a person buy the McMansion in the first place, all it takes is someone else buying an even bigger house to hurl the ego back to square one. Besides, living together is supposed to bring us together for all that sharing we mentioned. The bigger the house, the more possible it is for people to go off on their own—if we don't make a concerted effort to turn some of this separateness around.

As I'm sure you have heard, dinner together can help. It doesn't have to be fancy, doesn't have to take long—just long enough to eat something as healthy as you can muster, together. It is the quality of everything involved that counts. The highest quality you can find and afford. And that goes for people who live alone too. If Covid-19 taught us anything, it was that we do not have to have people in our homes to have good company in our lives. God bless Instacart, takeout, Zoom, and the human imagination. I hear the brain doesn't even know the difference between a real and an imaginary friend—someone you simply enjoy thinking about. So dine with whomever you like. And of course, it takes more than good takeout to make real-time relationships work, so let's take a look at those.

Quality Relationships

Relationships can matter as much as anything else to our overall quality of life. You know that if things are conflicted at home, the disturbance spills over into your work life, and vice versa. Round and round it goes, spiraling down, down, down. Anyone who has been through this knows how bad it feels, and we are shooting for great here. So, what can we do?

People tend to see conflict as bad, and sometimes it is, especially if that's all there is. But as with Victor, Sarah, and the trash bag example in the last chapter, we saw how that simple conflict was a vehicle through which they could take the relationship to a new and better place. In *Mediating Dangerously*, Kenneth Cloke puts it this way: "*Conflict is the voice of a new paradigm, a demand for change in a system that has outlived its usefulness.* The need for change always introduces itself in the form of conflict, including increased interpersonal conflict. The introduction of needed changes often reduces the level of conflict in an organizational or family system."[111]

COUPLES: Couples negotiate all the time, about everything. To own that fact opens up the opportunity to do it even better, to bring about the needed change. As before, it helps if we can listen well enough to repeat back, to confirm and affirm the other, as well as to be mindful that we are not just talking to hear ourselves talk: true, kind, necessary, beneficial, true, kind, necessary, beneficial . . . or at least do no harm.

Now, here is something else I don't know if you know. And since I really wish more people did know this, here goes: "Power infuses all relationships"—so says Hara Estroff Marano, in *Psychology Today,* and I agree.[112] The word *power* tends to have a negative connotation because when it's one-sided, as is too often the case, it is negative. We all want to matter in our own right. The issue is, once again, not about who spends how much time on what but about how much partners convey respect for the other's ideas and feelings, and a demonstrated willingness to be influenced by them. Experts agree that supporting the individual growth of the other is another great way to show the respect we all want and deserve. Personal growth is also a great way to introduce enough novelty in the relationship to keep the thing interesting and alive, which is good for the kids too.

KIDS: Evolutionary biologists and psychologists talk about parent–offspring conflict, which they say begins in the womb. Mom may look saintly on the outside, but she is engaged in a battle for nutrients with her unborn child, a battle that the fetus wages through its own secretion of hormones. When things don't go well, we get diabetes and blood pressure problems. When things do go well, everybody gives and gets, and it all works out. According to Steven Pinker, "The point of the theory is not that children want to take or that parents don't want to give; it's that children want to take *more* than what their parents want to give."[113]

We have already discussed this in the context of sibling rivalry at work. And we all know our brains help us to survive and thrive. So how can parents find room to breathe in the context of loving and growth-promoting relationships with their kids? The same ways we suggested in the adult-to-adult context. They treat them with respect and, in so doing, earn it in return.

We do not need to consider children mini-humans over whom we have dominion. Just as with adults, children want to matter in their own right. So the best practice is, once again, to convey respect for the child's ideas and feelings, a demonstrated willingness to be influenced by them, and full-blown support of their individual growth into a human being separate from their mom or dad. This is also a great way to ensure that the kids will actually be able to go off someday, happy and healthy on their own. You want that, right? Then you might even have some time for friends, which can be so good for the soul.

FRIENDS: When we were cave people, friendships supported our physical safety. In the words of philosopher Alain de Botton, "Now we have the police and the state for survival. So what are friends for? They are there to support us in our commitments, to guide us gently away from risks, and to help us to develop our thoughts and insights. The job has turned from physical to psychological."[114]

However, as more and more men, and then women, left their home bases for work outside the home, it seemed that more and more men and women turned to the couple relationship for what friendship used to provide. Who has time for friends? And how convenient! You don't even have to make arrangements. There you are, right there for each other, typically every day. Where it is working, please enjoy. Where it seems to be overburdening your relationship, it might be time to reach outside of the relationship to add one or some other friends in. Not just any old friends, though. Good-company friends. Mutually caring friendships, there for each other in good times and bad. Some people are not that good at being there for you when things are good, raising a question about whether they are or should be our friends. That said, truly good friends are good for the quality of your life and your health—and one of the sweetest, most important gifts you can give to yourself.[115]

YOURSELF: That's right, I mean here the quality of your relationship with yourself, upon which I believe everything else in your life rests. Said another way, our relationships in the external environment mirror our relationship to ourselves. This means that you should provide yourself with high-quality food and drink, as much as you can find and afford, as you would if you were having company, only in this case the "company" is you. It means you tuck yourself in at night with something soothing and go to bed early enough to get the rest you need, just the way you would with a child you love. It means that you take care of your body and your mind so both are as fit as they can be to support the highest quality of life for you, inside and out. I know that I am not the first to say this about caring for yourself, and you have likely heard it before, but I hope that you will consider it if you don't yet believe it yourself.

As you know, there are all kinds of apps, groups, and coaches to support you in any and all of the above. Even so, I understand that old habits die hard, and that to up-level to great in any one of these areas, let alone in a number of them, might seem daunting. So let's talk about change management. There is a lot we know now that can make it all work, and maybe even make it fun.

How People Change

Decades ago I read two authors who left indelible marks on me and my work. One was psychoanalyst Allen Wheelis, and the other was family therapist Salvadore Minuchin. I appreciated these authors because it felt to me that they were onto something at that time that few others were and thereby spoke to me in a way that the others did not. More specifically, they talked about action at a time when slow, slogging, insight-oriented psychotherapy seemed more in vogue. If I remember correctly, the Wheelis answer to how people change was "they just do." And I remember from Minuchin that somebody in the family had to change something. Minuchin didn't much care what it was; it could be their shoelaces or the chair they sat in, but something, anything, just to unfreeze the system that had them all so miserably stuck. With their help, I gradually crafted my own more action-oriented way of helping people to grow and change, with a best-of-both-worlds blend of insight and action, with quicker and better results.

There are times when it helps to go back to the formative years, but only as much as is necessary to get the job done. And the job is . . . to get to great in the present and future of work and life. So, for example, when one of my clients realized that at a tender young age he had been the "savior" in his dysfunctional family of origin, he also realized that to keep this glorification of himself (and his ego) alive, he would always be needing a dysfunctional environment to play the "savior" role in. This was an important awakening because sinking ships are not that much fun when your livelihood depends on them. To dig out of his attachment to the "savior" identity, he would have to plant and grow a new favorite version of himself. And for this he would have to take action that gave him the confidence to grow more and more into this new and better, happier, healthier, more productive person he wanted to become.

So, now I like to think of change management as gardening—not because I am a gardener, as I am not particularly, although my plants are green and tend to live a long time. Healthy plants were always important to me because I imagined that my clients would wonder how could I possibly take care of them if I couldn't take care of my plants. It is important that things flourish for the plants, the clients, and me. Remember what we said about how beneficial nature is for our health. And imagine my delight when I read Pollack and Cabane's article,[116] which explains the neurology of the brain as a garden, just like I said.

The "brain as garden" concept begins with the old saying that neurons that fire together wire together. That's why practice makes perfect, let's say, for playing the piano or riding a bike—neurons firing together, collaborating together, getting to know each other in a way that makes them so strong that we don't even have to think about whatever it is we are trying to do. New habits take root and grow, by the growth and development of neural connections that get watered and fertilized by firing and wiring together over and over again.

Equally as important is that neural connections that don't get watered die like weeds. We don't have to work hard to change bad habits. We just have to make sure we don't feed them. Eventually the neural connection will weaken, die, and get cleaned up when we sleep (for those of us who sleep—more on this later). For now, just as with the legend of the two warring wolves, the good one and the bad one, when the little boy asks which wolf wins, his grandfather responds, "The one you feed." New and better ways of living can grow and flourish with good care and time. And this, my friends, is the best way to answer the question of how people change. One foot in front of the other, one step at a time. Steps not so big that we are overwhelmed and shut down, and not so little that we are unmotivated and uninspired. One just-right-enough step at a time, on the road to great in work and life.

The exercise following our case example is called "wheel of life," originally created by pioneer in coaching Paul J. Meyer, and free online through the Coaching Tools Company,[117] to help us with where to begin in upgrading the quality of our own lives.

Case Example

Charlie is an accountant who was raised by wealthy parents who sent him to all the best private schools. As he did not perceive his parents to be particularly nice people, especially not to him, Charlie developed a whole constellation of ideas about how mean, wrong, and bad rich people were. He consequently did everything he could to make sure he didn't identify with that "class"—not a club he wanted to belong to. Literally. For example, although he was often invited to the yacht club with colleagues he actually liked, he shunned them in favor of working on his fixer-upper boat with a friend who was struggling with drugs. Charlie lived in an apartment that he said was practically "rat infested." Although I doubted that it was, let's just say it did not sound all that posh either. He suffered a series of broken marriages and unfulfilling relationships. And his relationships with his children were just as broken as everything else.

It took Charlie longer than most to get *grounded* in the belief that he didn't have to live quite like that to make sure that he was not like the parents he didn't respect. But he did *recognize* from the get-go that what needed to change was inside himself. Over time, as Charlie's internal environment became a warmer, more forgiving place, Charlie began to *explore* specific ways in which a better quality of life could be possible for him. His impressive *actions* included building a beautiful new house in a neighborhood full of nice people, with a lush and large garden he loves to tend.

Charlie's whole life is like a new garden he is tending, and now includes renewed relationships with his kids, who are also enjoying the new home and him. Charlie is *tackling* how he can generate and enjoy financial security in a way that does not make him feel and behave like "them."

Something tells me that after he gets through this knothole, he will be ready to add a fine woman in his life—as Charlie is *Getting to Great in Work and Life,* one foot in front of the other, everything in due time.

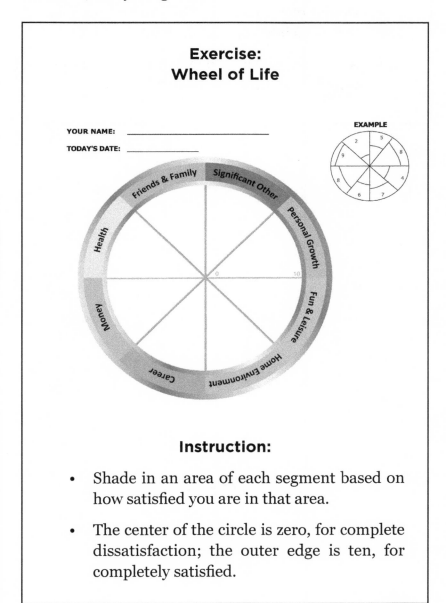

Exercise:
Wheel of Life

YOUR NAME: _____

TODAY'S DATE: _____

EXAMPLE

Instruction:

- Shade in an area of each segment based on how satisfied you are in that area.

- The center of the circle is zero, for complete dissatisfaction; the outer edge is ten, for completely satisfied.

- Next, draw a line across where you stopped shading, and write the number in.

- Do not overthink this. Use the first number that pops into your head. What do you see?

- Ask yourself which one of these categories would most affect all the rest.

What then is time? If no one asks me, I know what it is.
If I wish to explain it to him who asks, I do not know.
~ *Saint Augustine*

7
TYRANNY OF TIME

My Strong Suit

TIME IS MY STRONG SUIT. I can do time. Maybe it was those endless home-alone hours, when I was grounded, that made me as skilled as I am with time. Often I wrote books that I would sew up the middle with a big needle and some wool, after I colored the cover with crayons. Sometimes I was allowed out for a couple of hours on Saturday to meet my best friend, Barbara, for a Philly cheesesteak and a trip to Woolworth's five and dime—only after I finished dusting and vacuuming the house while everyone else was out doing what outside people do. The chores took much longer than they might have because there was more to do than just dust and vacuum. There was singing and dancing and talking to Grandmom Rose when I stopped by to dust her face on top of the TV. And since I had to fit all of that in and still meet Barbara at whatever time I said I would,

I had loads of opportunity to get good at managing—and enjoying—my "time," whatever that is.

Time is hard to understand. Although physicists define time as "the progression of events from the past to the present into the future,"[118] I prefer to go with Kant's idea that time is a form that the mind projects upon the external world, because if we are making it up in the first place, then we should be able to make it up in a way that works even better. Accordingly, this chapter will review four different kinds of time—*biological time, physical* or *clock time, psychological time,* and *timelessness time*—to see how we can optimize this all-day everyday thing we call *time*.

Biological Time

In 1729, a heliotrope (Latin for "turning toward the sun") in a dark room was found to fold and unfold its leaves in concert with the one in the garden that unfolded with the sunrise and folded again every night when the sun went down—as if the one that could not see the sun could tell time without it.[119] Subsequent experiments on plants and flowers and bugs and monkeys and mice and roaches showed that just about everything and everybody could tell time.

We know this biological internal clock as circadian rhythm, circadian pertaining to "day." It is a drummer whose beat we should march to more than we do. For example, there is the mental and physiological "post-lunch dip," that apparently has little if anything to do with lunch.[120] This is a good time to nap. We already talked about the benefits of naps, but do keep it short, say ten to twenty minutes, if you want to come out of it not feeling like you still need a nap. And we also don't want to interfere with our nighttime sleep, as "an estimated 50 to 70 million Americans have chronic (ongoing) sleep disorders."[121]

Companies that supply electricity and water can tell by when the lights go on and toilets get flushed how increasingly sleep-deprived we are.[122] People tend to steal time away from sleep for other things, without realizing how deadly this can be. There is reported to be more than double the risk of early death for people who cut their sleep from seven to five hours a night;[123] although sleeper beware—some research suggests that too much sleep, an increase to eight or more hours a night, can hurt you just as much, or could be a sign that something is not right and your doctor should be consulted.[124] So please, please take the time, and protect your time, to get the right sleep.

Easier said than done, you say. If you happen not to be sleeping so well, you don't really need yet another human being telling you to get some rest. Maybe you already have someone nagging you about it, but even if you don't, you may worry about it a lot yourself. And something is probably already worrying you so you can't sleep: "Not surprisingly, about 75 percent of cases of insomnia are triggered by some major stressor."[125] Then, on top of that, you may start worrying about how messed up you are going to be tomorrow when you have to perform and provide whatever it is that the world expects of you, with no sleep. Don't do that. Try this:

Get out of bed and sit somewhere warm and comfortable, readying yourself for an exploration of where the mind is *going* that is in the way of your *going to sleep*. As you feel yourself falling still, breathing in through the nose, out through the nose . . . you may begin to watch the thoughts that go by. What do these thoughts tell you about what the mind is doing instead of sleeping? If there is something you can do about whatever it is, you may decide whether it is something you can do now. If there is nothing you can do at this time—and usually there is not—you may decide to write something down to do at another time, and do something else entirely with this time, or return to your bed as one of a number of alternatives of what to do now. It is your time. You are in charge now.

This sense of agency can free you of some of the angst that is keeping you up at night, maybe even relax you enough to go to sleep if you want to, or not if you don't. When the mind begins to chastise that *you should be sleeping* during this exercise, remember that thoughts are not facts. Just let these thoughts come and then let them go. Gently remind yourself that you were not sleeping anyway, and will eventually figure out how to manage your sleep time. And please consider the potential of a regular daily meditation practice to help you to sleep. This really can help.[126]

Physical Time

It was always about the sun, moon, planets, and stars. From the National Institute of Standards and Technology,[127] we learn that as far back as 20,000 years ago, Ice-Age hunters in Europe were scratching lines and holes in sticks, possibly to keep track of the days between phases of the moon. In Ancient Egypt, by around 5,000 years ago, there were calendars, two of them. Since life and agriculture depended on the annual flooding of the Nile, it was important to know when the floods would begin. The first calendar was the twelve-month lunar calendar. The second, for administrative purposes, had 365 days, i.e., twelve months with thirty days and then five days tacked on at the end. These last five were considered the unlucky days, so it was recommended that one not mess with anything that mattered much during those days. Many of us still don't "work" during the last five days of the year. Some things don't change.

By about 400 BCE, the two calendars became one. By 239 BCE, there was an attempt to include a leap year, which did not actually happen until 23 BCE when the Romans reformed the Egyptian calendar. So that little improvement took 216 years to implement, just to put things in perspective for people who think things today don't move fast enough. But the overall point is that we created time to help us—not to torture us the way we have let it, practically right from the start. From the ancient Hindu *Bhagavad Gita,* written thousands of years ago: "I am come as Time, the waster of peoples, Ready for the hour that ripens to their ruin."[128]

Come on, now. Who's in charge here? Are we going to let this abstract thing we made up, that no one can even define, define our lives? But there are only twenty-four hours in a day, you say; what can we do about that?

We don't have to do anything about that because when we are practicing good company (good food, sleep, people), we increase our energy, which increases the amount and quality of what we get done. Who needs more hours? There are plenty enough hours in the day when we are spending them right. To test this for yourself, you can draw two pie charts. The first is your *real-time chart*, sectioned off into how you actually spend your time. Here are some sample categories: work, family, friends, hobbies, Netflix, reading, chores, eating, sleeping, exercising, meditating, sex, miscellanea. Feel free to make up your own. Now take a look. Does your pie chart look right to you? For example, how many hours are you sleeping? The National Sleep Foundation recommends that you, as an adult, get between seven and nine hours of sleep.[129] Are you? What about the other categories?

When you are finished, you can make an *ideal pie chart* to reflect the adjustments and improvements that you would like to make. And then, if you care to, post copies of your *ideal pie* in the zones of your life represented on your chart. Why? What is the point of all this pie? The point is *attention*; that is to say, to direct your attention to that which is good. Philosopher Ken Wilbur suggests that the reason we may feel pressured to do something is because we want to do it more than we may know. [130] You get that? *You want to! So give it your attention*. Talk about increasing energy. Do you have any idea how much energy you waste trying to decide whether you want to do . . . whatever it is? There, it's settled, and now you have freed up all of that energy for other things, as if you have just given yourself extra hours in the day.

And if you really don't want to be doing whatever it is, then fix your pie, post it, give that your attention—and see what happens. Attention again? So, what is attention? From William James: "Everyone knows what attention is. It is the taking possession by the mind, in clear and vivid form, of one out of what seem several simultaneously possible objects or trains of thought. It implies withdrawal from some things in order to deal effectively with others, and is a condition which has a real opposite in the confused, dazed, scatterbrained state."[131]

The opposite of attention is a messed-up state of mind. Bravo, William James. Moreover, the brain is always in "ready mode"—that is, ready to turn the "spotlight" on something it chooses to pay attention to. Professor of psychiatry John Ratey claims, "Attention is much more than simply taking note of incoming stimuli. It involves a number of distinct processes, from filtering out perceptions, to balancing multiple perceptions, to attaching emotional significance to them."[132]

In short, if it feels good, (you will) do it. If you have an area in your life you want to expand in time and importance, be sure to conjure up a mental/emotional image of what's so good about making it bigger. Even if you think you are doing it for someone else, there must be some kind of reward in that for you, or you would not be trying to expand it in the first place. Whatever it is, bring it to the front of your brain, and tag it emotionally when you look at that piece of your pie.

Likewise for an area you want to shrink. If you even keep it in the chart, look at it and tell yourself why it is now only a sliver. Notice that no one is telling you exactly what to do or not do with your life. This is about you taking charge, learning how to mess with your own head so that no one else can. You may also want to check out other time-management techniques if this one is not for you. They are everywhere online.[133] I am wondering, though, whether you put slices in your pies for all the time you may spend *ruminating* (about the past) or *worrying* (about the future)—our next-up type of time, *psychological time*.

Psychological Time

To this point, we have been talking mostly about chunking up the present and future moments of our lives, about real-time everyday things we need or want to do or not do during the course of a day. Many people spend a good part of that time in some other time zone altogether without even knowing it because, believe it or not, humans have a great deal of discretion over time, even if it doesn't feel that way to you yet.

Consider the Amazon Pirahã tribe. Pirahã people supposedly live without time, except to describe whether something is in their immediate experience in a now-you-see-it-now-you-don't-and-that's-all-that-matters kind of way.[134] And what about the South American Aymaras?

They put their future behind them and their past in front of them.[135] Think about it. Makes sense in a way. We can see the past because it already happened but not the future because it hasn't. Good for them. And the Navajo. As one psychiatrist put it, "What I learned from the Navajo is that paying a lot of attention to time is a culturally arbitrary value. Once I realized that, I had choice as to the degree to which I wanted to be a slave to time."[136]

Clock time is useful and practical; psychological time is something else. Clock time is good for making appointments and plans. Psychological time can be the "identification with the past and continuous compulsive projection into the future,"[137] instead of just returning to the present once the practical matters—informed by the past or future—have been taken care of. We know this as ruminating (past) and worrying (future), and it hurts when it has outlived its useful purpose and gone to excess. I find it helps to ask yourself a simple question when you're caught up in knots and don't feel like bothering everyone you know about it: *Is there something to be done here?* If so, do it. If not, cut it out—and get back to what you are supposed to be doing in that moment of your life.

I get abducted by the future, which is not always the best use of my time. After all, how much can we really know now about who and how we are going to be and feel then? And wonderful things really are possible without planning at all. Take my children. It is true that I paid great attention to planning for *their* future happiness, but I do not remember ever considering what they would mean to *me* in this "future moment" of my own life. An attentional bonus, I suppose you could say. But that's about me. What about you? Toward which tense, past or future, does your mind tend to stray when your attention goes off on its own?

It would be good for you to take the time to explore that and, in so doing, begin to train the mind to take control of where and how your mind spends your time.

Time is not the absolute we tend to think it is. Again, it is to a considerable degree all in our heads. This is what we mean by psychological time. Some people think, feel, and behave as if there is *never* enough time. Others, with the same number of actual hours in their day, are able to use well and enjoy the time that there is. Relaxation makes a difference. You can prove this to yourself if you have a timepiece with a second hand. Sit comfortably, with your eyes closed, in a position that allows you to see the timepiece easily when you open your eyes, without much movement of your head. Now falling still, and becoming aware of your breath, gently in through the nose and out through the nose, each time the mind wanders, gently bring the attention back to the breath.

Once you feel still and relaxed, you may gently open your eyes and look at the second hand on your watch. For those first couple of seconds, did the second hand seem to slow down? To hesitate? Or maybe even to stop altogether? As Deepak Chopra has said, "Once you have had the experience of seeing a watch stop, you will never again doubt that time is a product of perception."[138] There is a movement called the Society for the Deceleration of Time, with a website and members all over Central Europe trying to slow down time, including a group for slow sex.[139] (Someone always thinks about that.) I don't get the sense, though, that these groups are promoting free time as much as they are promoting full engagement in whatever we are doing with our time—meaningful time. But where can we find the time that is "free of busy activity"? Which brings us to our fourth and final type of time: *timelessness time.*

Timelessness Time

Slowness guru Carl Honore talked about a meditation retreat he attended:

> The meditation clearly has an effect . . . even on the fastest, most stress-addled mind. . . . By Saturday night, I notice that I am taking more time to eat and brush my teeth. I have started walking, instead of running, up the stairs. . . . By Sunday night . . . [m]y mind is learning to be quiet and still for longer. I feel less impatient and hurried. . . . By the end of the weekend, ideas for work are bursting up from my subconscious mind like fish jumping in a lake. Before returning to London, I sit in the car scribbling them down.[140]

How can we keep our lives from becoming one big mindless, mushy blur of time and attention spent on too many of the wrong things in too many of the wrong ways—like on money, let's say, which is coming up next? In other words, how can we beat the clock and take back our lives? One suggestion is that we pause between activities to keep the mind clear, focused, and well directed for things that matter. At the end of this chapter, you will find an exercise to help with this, called *focus and release*.

Case Example

Rebecca is a high-powered business executive with a good marriage and a family of origin that is dysfunctional, emotionally and financially, in ways that just break her heart. Rebecca reached out to me to feel better without really changing anything much in her way of doing and being with them. Her **grounding** in the idea that she could address her concern for her family any differently did not come easily at first. Eventually she **recognized** that although she could not change her family, she could change herself and her ways of caring about them.

As Rebecca began to **explore** alternative ways of doing and being with her family, she experimented with time. She wanted to "spend time" with her family but realized that what kind of time that should be was not carved in stone. Given how stressful she found their longer visits, when Rebecca realized that time was a construct of her own mind, the **action** she took, with good success, was to try out more frequent visits for shorter periods of time. Rebecca is **tackling** her other habits of giving to her family—let's say with money—in the same way she did with time. Rebecca is *Getting to Great in Work and Life*, still with understandable sorrow for those she loves, but with less time- and energy-draining guilt than she ever thought possible.

Exercise:
Focus and Release

Have you ever noticed how hard it can be to stop yourself when you are engaged in an activity and have run out of time? How much of whatever we might be thinking and feeling about the job we didn't finish lives on to contaminate the activity we move on to next? And how much attention are we even paying to the activity we are doing in the moment we are doing it? One improperly attended activity after another can ruin the enjoyment and results of that activity and burden you with an overall sense of dissatisfaction that doesn't need to be there.

This exercise is designed to help you learn to focus on the activity at hand, and then to put it down so you can pick something else up—and move from one activity to another with fuller attention and the satisfaction that goes with it.

To Practice:

- At the beginning of an activity, briefly close your eyes or simply gaze downward, breathing in through the nose, out through the nose.

- Now anchor (focus) your attention right on the activity, e.g., where your fingers hit the keyboard, the pen touches the paper, the paintbrush touches the woodwork, where the sound of a speaker's voice hits your ear. Be there.

- At the end of each activity, deliberately put down whatever tools or objects you may have in your hands, and again breathe in through the nose, out through the nose, until you feel that you are present in the time and space that you are meant to be in.

- Now you may say quietly or silently to yourself, *"And now I release this activity."* Even if the task has not been completed to the extent that you had planned, you have released it for the present time, and moved on in a clear, strong, ready-for-anything way to whatever comes next.

The real measure of your wealth is how much you'd be
worth if you lost all your money.
~ Unknown

8
CONCERNING MONEY

Money Shame

YES, THAT'S RIGHT, I want to talk about money, and have
been intrigued for years about why most other people don't.
A couple of decades ago, at a gathering of women who met
every month to dine and discuss a variety of topics, I asked
if we could discuss money sometime. The backstory here
is that we actually started out as an investment club, but
morphed to "dine and discuss" when dot-coms went belly
up. Even as an investment club, though, we talked more
about companies than about our own money. And I knew
I wanted to write about this taboo someday, so I took a
chance with them to see what I could learn.

"I don't want to talk about money; it makes me feel bad"
was all that was said, and that would have been that, except
that the woman who said that could not attend the next
meeting. The following month, in her absence, I raised it

again, asking, "If you picked up a chapter on 'spending' [as I was calling it then], what would you expect the chapter to be about?"

"Why we do it," came the reply from the head of the table. Why we do what? Spend, I suppose, but that is only a guess because at that point they all stood up, took their dishes to the kitchen, and disappeared, one by one, smoothly into the night. Duly noted, and I did cherish these women, so I decided to just leave it alone with them from then on. Still, I wondered what all the fuss was about.

My maternal grandmother wholly owned and operated a successful business back in the days when not a lot of women did. She had to have known something about money. And my mother ran the numbers for a good-sized payroll for our family business, out loud, without a calculator, at the kitchen table as if she were speaking in tongues. And I cannot recall having a single conversation with either one of these women, nor anyone else for that matter, about how I would take care of myself when I grew up. Although, now that I think of it, to her credit, Grandmom Bessie did play Monopoly with me a lot.

Still, I can't help but wonder how much more financial success I would have allowed myself had someone told me that I was supposed to grow up to be a woman of great philanthropy and means in my own right—or if anyone had talked to me directly about money at all so I would have thought it was more okay to talk and think about it myself. I also know from my work that I am not the only person with a self-limiting money mindset, in both earning and spending, even though, except for my clients, I don't hear people talk about these kinds of things very much. Again . . . well, it's taboo.

Maybe some parents tend not to talk with their kids

about money because their parents didn't talk with them.[141] I also imagine some parents don't want the kids to know about family finances because they are afraid it will worry the kids—and get out the door. Little pitchers have big ears, and mouths. Do you really want your neighbors to know your net worth or your income? And if not, why not? Shame and fear, that's why not. Shame over what you don't have, shame over what you do have, and fear over who will think and do what about what you do or don't have. There it is again: *the look.*

From the Whitehall Studies on social position and health: "The Whitehall studies support the Hobbesian view of human nature as a war of all against all. To survive and prosper you have to do better than others. In a world of scarce resources, survival depends on constantly striving to outdo your fellow human beings."[142] Shameful indeed to even consider such a thing about ourselves, let alone to expose it to anyone else. The Whitehall Studies began in 1967, before we had Facebook and FOMO, but you get the idea. Humans are comparing animals, as "keeping up with the Joneses" affirms.

Developmental psychologist Erik Erikson gave us another important reason we may feel shame about money. That is, the shame one feels when exposed as being unable to take care of oneself.[143] But who even knows? Who's even looking? Everyone. Everyone is watching everyone else—about money. Neuroimaging techniques have shown how much the brain of one *"Homo economicus"* delights or despairs when it notices that another *"Homo economicus"* may have received fewer or more euros, respectively.[144] Other money researchers use the term "have-mores" to indicate that "disparity-in-wealth problems" exist as much *within* groups of "haves" and "have-nots" as between them.[145]

Welcome to "Rank Theory":

> An evolved capacity for the recognition and acceptance of rank difference in social groups . . . establishes precedence in granting right of access to indispensable resources such as territory, food, and potential mates. It follows that gaining rank is associated with elevated mood and losing rank with depressed mood. The adaptive function of the depression, according to rank theory, is to facilitate losing and to promote accommodation to the fact that one has lost . . . to prevent the loser . . . from suffering further injury . . . and reduce his level of aspiration . . . on the basis that he who fights and runs away lives to fight another day.[146]

"He who fights and runs away will live to fight another day." Demosthenes, I believe.[147] So, if things did not work out as you expected (true for a lot of people these days), take your lumps, lick your wounds, and figure out how to regain some sense of standing within your family, your community, and most of all, within yourself—so you don't get unduly depressed. This is a mindset shift you can accomplish, either on your own or with some help. Try it and see how it works. And please know that what you don't have, or what you might have lost, likely does not matter the way you might think it does. Thoughts are not facts. You are not your money. And your money is not you.

Then what is money, and what is it for?

Why Money?

Money doesn't buy happiness—not unless the money satisfies some unmet food-or-shelter-type basic need.[148]

No matter how many studies emerge to convince us that unless we are starving and homeless, money all by itself is unlikely to make us any happier than we already are, we keep thinking that it will.

Who is responsible for this? We are. We have been buying and selling things ever since we left the trees: "amber, beads, cowries, drums, eggs, feathers, gongs, hoes, ivory, jade, kettles, leather, mats, oxen, pigs, quartz, rice, salt, thimbles, umiacs, vodka, wampum, yarns and zappozats (decorated axes)."[149] We chose things for barter (my axe, which I make better than you do, for your spear, which I don't have time to make because I am busy making axes, and your spears are better than I could make them anyway, even if I had the time, which I don't); for their durability; for how easily they could be transported and stored—and for status.

These ancient currencies were also used to pay for crimes committed, for brides taken away from service to their own fathers, or for taxes and tribute to rulers. Currency is good to have in case you need it for a variety of purposes, especially for status. The North American potlatch is a competitive gift-giving ceremony for status. The more one gives, the more status one gets; the more status one gets, the more resources one has to give, so the more status one gets—and so on. Money begets money. Our ancestors had to have money to get money, and status.

Sound familiar? Maybe you have been to a baby shower that felt like a competitive gift-giving event. Internally and externally driven FOMO and *the look* all over the place—largely to seek status that we think will make us feel safe, although we do have some other values. Distributive justice matters a lot too. In study after study, people would rather accept absolutely nothing than reward unfairness by accepting an offer perceived to be unfair.[150] The brain's reward circuitry gets nearly as jazzed up about being treated fairly as it would if you got to eat food that you had been craving all day.[151]

So, if we pare this down to *status, fairness,* and the *avoidance of shame* as major factors driving our money madness, it becomes easier to understand all the fuss. People are driven to want at least as much as—preferably more than—relevant others in their external environment, which then, on some level possibly not conscious, feels not fair. People also want more than themselves! More, more, more, and at the same time they want it all to be fair. Can you see the problem here? Psychologists also talk about a hedonic treadmill, which means that because we adapt, the thrill wears off, so we always have to have more, more, more. This is exactly what the experts say is going on with spendaholics, only it backfires: "Spending addiction is an attempt to try to 'buy' happiness—to feel admired, to feel accepted, to feel empowered, to push away troubling feelings, like self-doubt or self-disappointment—and can risk ruining everything you hold dear."[152]

No wonder so many people are so stressed out about money. Just as with time, we forget that money did not create us. We created money, to help us survive and thrive. And yet, somehow, instead of our being in charge of money— or, even better, having a healthy, respectful relationship with money—we have let both time and money outright bully us. The consequences are serious and real.

Money Stress

We know that Covid-19 hit a lot of people hard financially. But it is also important to remember that money angst was there before Covid. The American Psychological

Association's (APA) "Stress in America 2019" study reported that stress levels "remain relatively constant year to year."[153] Still, in 2019, 60 percent of adults reported being significantly stressed by money, second only to work (64 percent), and who knows how much of the work stress was driven by or impacted by stress about money? In November 2019, Forbes reported it even higher: during boom times, no less, only 29 percent of Americans considered themselves "financially healthy," which means that 71 percent did not.[154] Then, in 2020, as if money weren't already worrisome enough, the world upended and things got worse. From the APA's 2020 "Stress in the Time of Covid" report: "The economy is reported as a significant source of stress by 7 in 10 adults (70%)."[155] And the National Endowment for Financial Education reported nine in ten Americans feeling anxious about money.[156]

And why does this matter?

Money stress matters in the context of the environmental mismatch theory we have already discussed. To review, the brain doesn't know we are not on the savanna anymore. It doesn't know we are not going to actually be eaten or starve. All the brain knows is that we feel like our survival is threatened, so fight or flight kicks into high gear, and there it gets stuck. Neuroscientist Robert Sapolsky talks about "adventitious pain," the psychological stress that we humans are smart enough to invent in our heads:

> If you are a zebra and a lion has leapt out and ripped your stomach open, and you are in pain and you are running for your life, the things you do with your body are wonderful, are exactly what you want to happen in order to survive. But if you were a human suffering from adventitious pain, the key thing is

your body does the exact same thing, and when it does that, and if it does that for a long time, disease will arise.[157]

Do take a look at his *Why Zebras Don't Get Ulcers* book,[158] which is organized by ailment so you can go directly to the one you may have reason to care about.

The point is that it's not what actually happens as much as *what the mind makes of what happens* that matters—that adventitious suffering that we invent all on our own. And all the thinking, thinking, thinking . . . It would all be over quickly—the stress response—and do no harm, if not for all of that. People have known for a long, long time that it is pretty much all in our heads. Maybe you don't like that I said that; but people like the Buddha have known this all along. [159] The Buddha talks about two arrows. The first arrow is the pain that cannot be helped. Stuff happens. The second arrow, more painful than the first, is all of that suffering that would not even exist without your mind's help. All of the arrows seem to be pointing to the mind-body relation, with the undisciplined mind largely responsible for the trouble.

As before, everything is connected to everything else. So, for example, especially for those lacking health insurance, treatment for illness may be delayed or nonexistent. Conditions worsen, productivity suffers, affecting ability to work, which compounds the financial worry, causing more stress, worsening whatever the ailment may be, and so on. As for the social withdrawal and relationship tensions, it is not hard to see here how the shame we talked about earlier could play a part. That is, since people who feel internal shame are often ashamed to feel ashamed, there can be a turning inward, or a lashing out at others in the external environment for what we have called *the look*. As we discussed, *the look* is about what we imagine others are thinking about us that makes us feel bad.

It does not have to be this way. And, yes, I have had times in my life, as a child and as an adult, when I worried about money, so I know. Still, there are things we can do, beginning with **grounding** in this belief that it does not have to be this way, and **recognizing** that fitness requires knowing who we are and what we are made of on the inside. Let's hear it from Holocaust survivor and psychoanalyst Viktor Frankl: "Forces beyond your control can take away everything you possess except one thing, your freedom to choose how you will respond to the situation."[160]

If financial woes exist in your life right now, you can do some **exploring** of potential areas of control, and design some corresponding **actions** that will include **tackling** whatever might come up and threaten to get in the way. I am not saying that you will necessarily feel great immediately, although you might. But at least contrasted with what it could feel like if you don't take control of what you can control, it could be great if you do.

Money Mindset

We said before that mindfulness is "paying attention in a particular way: on purpose, in the present moment, and nonjudgmentally."[161] Applying this kind of attention to our finances is how we can reassure ourselves that we are doing the best we can. Recalling Erikson's take on how much we need to feel we are taking care of ourselves, I believe that this is less about a dollar amount than knowing that we exerted some control over our lives, and behaved as financially responsible as we could. I also believe that the first step in taking charge of our financial lives is to get over ourselves and *talk about it*. Here are some suggestions.

TALK: One study found that 43 percent of Americans don't know what their spouses earn, which likely means—I'm just guessing—that there is a money-talk taboo in the household.[162] Another study found that arguing about money is a leading cause of divorce.[163] It makes sense that when money matters are unspeakable, eventually they blow up. Open talk about money may also help people make sure they are getting their due salary. After all, it is hard to learn what other people are making if there are sanctions against talking about it.

LEARN: There is much to learn about college funds, retirement plans, debt management, how to prepare a budget. Sometimes people are reluctant to ask for advice from family, friends, or professionals because they think they are supposed to already know. There goes *the look*, and shame, again. But knowledge is power, so it is worth accepting and then tackling these self-limiting forces as much as we can.

GOOD COMPANY: Cultivate relationships with people who want to talk about money, for support and to share ideas on tips, techniques, and goals. Churches have finance groups, and finance meetups are available online. There are faith-based and secular trainings specifically for couples, and for parents to learn how to educate their kids about money. All of these learning opportunities are also opportunities to meet like-minded people who want to support each other in their money anxieties and, even better, help overcome them together, and even grow their wealth. Many young people are doing that now, forming groups to support each other in making their for-profit and nonprofit dreams come true.

PROFESSIONAL HELP: As women's economic power has grown through employment outside of the home, for some men there can be an identity shift—or even a threat—that not everyone is skilled at managing effectively. And then there are the more general individual stress symptoms of anxiety, depression, shame, disillusionment, hopelessness—understandable, and deeply painful, when financial times are tough. For anyone who is suffering, again, put *the look* and shame to the side, and get what you need; the sooner, the better. Depression, especially, lifts much easier the earlier it is treated, before it becomes more like a way of life.

RELATIONSHIP-BUILDING FOR YOUR MONEY AND YOU: Once you have figured out some ways you might modify how you regard your money, to stay on that track—just like with the *inner critic*—you will have to *make friends with your money*. Psychotherapist and money relationships author Olivia Mellan suggested imagining that your money and you are being interviewed on Oprah about your relationship.[164] When I first did this exercise (which you will find here at the end of this chapter) my money spoke to me about respect. In the words of personal-finance expert Suze Orman, "Money . . . is drawn to those who welcome it, those who respect it. Wouldn't you rather be with people who respect you. . . . Your money feels the same way."[165]

My money was not actually complaining that I did not respect it, per se. Rather, my dear money said, "It seems like you respect me more than you respect yourself." That was years ago when I worried about how well I would be able to take care of myself—a time when, lacking financial confidence, I could probably have treated myself a little better and saved a little less. So I told my money I was sorry that I did not allow myself to enjoy it and trust it to be there for me. Maybe it would be better for me and for us, and for the country too, if I spent a little more and saved a little less, which over the years I have done. Oddly enough, as my confidence grew, so did my money, which is exactly what the mindset gurus would predict. The external environment is a mirror image of the internal environment. How true in this case.

Case Example

Patrick liked fine things: cars, homes, clothes, shoes, wine, etc. The proceeds from the sale of a business kept him in these things until they didn't anymore. By the time Patrick reached out to me, he had an uninspiring mid-level management job and a question about whether he would be able to support that kind of lifestyle for the rest of his life. We tapped into Patrick's nostalgia for an earlier, simpler time in his life to *ground* him in the belief that he did not have to spend the rest of his life on the hedonic treadmill. It didn't have to be like that. Patrick *recognized* that a better match between his more deeply held internal values and yearnings and the external environment in which he lived would bring him a more satisfying life. As I watched Patrick *explore* the ways in which he could simplify his life, and then take *action* to make it so, I was filled with admiration for both Patrick and his wise and kind wife.

Especially around the time of Covid, Patrick had to *tackle* the push and pull between his ego's demands and his own values. He is also aware of the strength of his marriage and personal resilience, and is taking practical and mindset steps to redefine himself as someone whose worth is not only attached to money. Patrick is *Getting to Great in Work and Life* by other, more satisfying and sustainable means.

Real peace will arise spontaneously
When your mind becomes free
Of attachments,
When you know that the objects of the world
Can never give you what you really want.
(*Theragatha*)[166]

Exercise:
Relationship-Building for Your Money and You

A wise mentor once said to me, "We have to take care of those we count on to take care of us." Have you thought of your money as existing to take care of you? Have you thought of yourself as endowed with the right and responsibility to take care of it, so that it can take care of you? What kind of relationship do you have with your money?

This exercise is designed to help you identify who you are in relation to your money, and to begin to assess how happy and healthy you believe that relationship to be.

To Practice:

- Find a quiet spot, make yourself comfortable, closing your eyes or simply gazing downward, and open to the sound around you to connect with one of the senses, to settle down your busy mind.

- And now imagine that you are on a daytime talk show having a "true, kind, necessary, beneficial" conversation with someone you are intimately involved with about what it's like to be in a relationship with you—only, that person is your money.

- The ground rule is that neither of you can argue with the other's point of view. Today we are here to listen and learn. Half of America is watching. What will you tell your money about what it's like to be in a relationship with it?

- Now it is your money's turn to talk. What is your money going to say about what it's like to be in a relationship with you?

- What do you think you two can work out to improve your relationship—and your life— going forward?

Play is the exultation of the possible.
~ *Martin Buber*

9
POWER OF PLAY

Not My Strong Suit?

BACK WHEN WE WERE TALKING about *time*, I said that time was my strong suit. For the same reason that time is, I could say that *play* is not. But I am not so sure about that because it depends on how we define "play"—whether we think I actually played my way through all of those home-alone years. After my father died, there were two reasons I was still not allowed out. One was that I was in the middle of the punishment for the most recent episode of speaking truth to power. The other was that in our religion, we were supposed to cover the mirrors and not go out to play for a period of at least thirty days, which I honored.

When the thirty days were up, I was allowed out, but was not really playing the way other kids do. What I remember is writing, as I always did, only this time I was writing dead-dad songs that I would play on my guitar in the backseat of my friend's dad's car. My friend told me that she had asked her father what they should do about me, and that he said, "Just be there for her; she'll figure it out."

Well, here I am still writing about my dead dad. But would you call it "playing"? What if I told you that I wake up in the morning happy to know that after I help my clients to transform their lives, I will be writing to you, my reader. What if I told you that when I sit down to write, it is like solving a puzzle—arranging my ideas and research materials, then figuring out how they will fit and flow together. What if I told you that when I write I feel joyful, filled with meaning and purpose, actively engaged in deep thought, socially engaged with you, and iterative, as I experiment with a repeatable chapter format, hoping to improve it for you along the way?

Would you say that sounds like playing? The Lego Foundation might, as these are the five characteristics of "play" they list on their website: actively engaging, meaningful, socially interactive, joyful, iterative.[167] Now, you might say, "Yeah, but we are not really interacting, you and I." But then I would say, "Yeah, but my brain doesn't know that because to me we are," and I do hope that you, my dear reader, actually will talk back to me someday. For now, though, consider this Warren Beatty quote I found online: "You've achieved success in your field when you don't know whether what you're doing is work or play." Sounds good to me, and entirely possible as more and more people align their true nature (internal environment) with the activities they pursue (external environment). I also want you to know that it feels as good as it sounds, but contrary to popular opinion, play is not just for the purpose of feeling good. So let's take a closer look at the purpose of play.

Purpose of Play

According to stress-management guru Joe Robinson,

When you're stressed, the brain's activated emotional hub, the amygdala, suppresses positive mood, fueling a self-perpetuating cycle of negativity. Play can break you out of that straitjacket. It's the brain's reset button. This tonic we write off as trivial is a crucial engine of well-being. In its low-key, humble way, play yanks grownups out of their purposeful sleepwalk to reveal the animating spirit within. You are alive, and play will prove it to you.[168]

Harvard researchers found that play not only relieves stress but also improves brain function, stimulates the mind, boosts creativity, improves relationships, and builds energy and resistance to disease.[169] So, if it's that good, how come we don't play more? Why is play such a guilty pleasure for some, or a waste of time for others? There is a saying that if something tastes good, it must be bad for you. Maybe this applies to play. Maybe we think that because play is fun, it must not be good for us. Here is why that would be wrong:

The ability to enjoy an activity is a survival trait. Sex is fun because seeking it is adaptive. People who don't like sex have a harder time finding mates and having kids. In general, enjoying an activity is a hardwired response that causes the brain to seek out that activity. If these essential behaviors weren't enjoyable, we might forget to do them. On these grounds, it seems that play must have an adaptive purpose, providing some survival advantage.[170]

In other words, the ones who thought sex was fun did it more and, therefore, had more babies who might also think sex is fun, and so on. Reproductive success may be one of the functions of play, but not the only one. Some researchers list thirty functions of play.[171] There is one type of play that I find to be the most interesting and important for us here: *social play.*

Social Play

Social play is one of the three types of play commonly recognized by researchers:[172]

- Object play (basketball)

- Locomotor play (running)

- Social play (pretending)

About 80 percent of mammals engage in social play; so do some birds, fish, and reptiles.[173] They are not us, though. We humans are the ultra-socials.[174] If necessity is the mother of invention, then climatic changes, or Mother Nature, necessitated our invention of interdependence and the social brain that grew big, flexible, and complex enough to pull it off.[175] As we discussed before, at some point our ancestors couldn't just climb up a tree to hide from predators or get food. There hardly were any trees anymore, and besides, we had to stand our ground, ready to kill and take care of each other, or we would be meat. So we had to develop ways to temper aggression within the group. We assumed rights, roles, and responsibilities. We made friends to help us cooperate and compete. And the more friends we made, the more people we interacted with in general, the bigger and smarter the social brain became. Play was instrumental all along.

Bear cubs who played during summer months were found to have lowered cortisol levels and to be more likely to survive the winter.[176] So either the lower cortisol levels facilitated resilience or the cubs who were healthier in the first place were more likely to play. Either way, play is good, and activates the brain to signal epinephrine, norepinephrine, and dopamine—associated with attention, action, learning, plasticity, motivation, and a group of capacities known as the four *F*s: fight, flight, fright, and fornication. As Dutch historian and culturalist Johan Huizinga suggested in his classic book *Homo Ludens* (1949), "If play serves some behavioral or evolutionary function, then the neural circuits of the brain involved in motivation and reward should be active during its occurrence."[177] Science now substantiates that they are, from the earliest days of our lives.

Child's Play

Play is voluntary; that's what makes us feel free when we play, if it really is play. Sure, there are rules, but if little kids don't like the rules, they can quit. Before that, babies are playing freely, freely exploring their worlds, during their first six months of life. More developed child's play—especially social fantasy play with its make believe, trial and error, experimentation, role play, rehearsals, and practice—may be forerunner to later innovation and problem-solving creativity and leadership. But what most captured my attention in researching this subject is the development of self-control and empathy that is made possible through play, and the primacy of means over ends in child's play.

Psychologists used to think that if an ability was hooked to survival, it was innate and could not be changed. Now we know that we are interdependent not only with each other, but with our environment as well. In other words, "Organisms affect their environment (e.g., by choosing and then 'furnishing their niches'), and environments, in turn, affect the organism (e.g., by changing behaviors to meet the particular demands of a setting)."[178]

There it is in a nutshell, the essence of my work and this book. From our opening line: *A great life depends on a great fit between who we are and the environments in which we work and live.* And here's what we know now: *We. Can. Do. This.* We can tinker with things, internal and external, to make a great difference in our lives. And we can do this through play: "Whether it is raucous or quiet, physical or mental, social or solitary, the act of playing seems to open the brain to possibilities. It is perhaps one of the best tools we have for developing our brains in ways that can help us learn how to survive in an unpredictable world."[179]

Child's play is a vehicle through which we grow to be human. By around age four, kids understand that other kids have ideas and desires too, possibly different from their own. This knowledge helps them to learn the art of controlling impulses that might alienate others with whom they wish to play, and the art of bonding with others who appreciate being understood and cared about. We may say it is the beginnings of what businesspeople call "know, like, and trust," only in this case it is an end in itself. Through play, a child learns mastery of life and living, a sense of mastery that is predominantly enjoyed for its own sake—and what I believe Erikson meant when he talked about how much we need to know that we can take care of ourselves.

So, adults beware. Play for children has shifted so far away from free play to more structured play that experts worry about concurrent rises in mental health issues and inhibited cognitive growth. The shift as well to more goal-oriented, winning-and-losing play can undo the stress-reducing benefits of play. So does pressure to play at things that in no way match or express the true nature of the child. Play works best when it is engaging and unstressed. This applies to adults as well.

Adult Play

Desmond Morris, the sociobiologist who wrote *The Naked Ape,* said that adult play "is what gives us all our greatest achievements—art, literature, poetry, theatre, music and scientific research."[180] So play is not only good for stress reduction, emotional and physical health, and cognitive development, but also good for the health and development of our culture itself. Play is also good for love and work. Let's start with love.

LOVE: Wikihow, which defines itself as "how-to instructions you can trust," offers ten pages of tips and techniques on role-playing for couples, with pictures.[181] Not your cup of tea? That's okay. Just know that both men and women find playfulness an attractive quality in a long-term mate, a quality found to be associated with positive emotions that are more fun and better for us overall than their opposite.[182] In the beginning of relationships, play, humor, and flirting can help ease some of the awkwardness in getting to know each other. *For longer-term couples,*

> Take play out of the mix and, like a climb up the oxygen-poor "death zone" of Mount Everest, the relationship becomes a survival endurance contest. Without play skills, the repertoire to deal with inevitable stresses is narrowed. Even if loyalty, responsibility, duty, and steadfastness remain, without playfulness there will be insufficient vitality left over to keep the relationship buoyant and satisfying.[183]

Fortunately, some people know that, especially after the early lust subsides, a relationship without some levity can be deadly. They know what to do: for example, body play (dancing), object play (golf), social play (dining with friends), pretend play (role play), narrative play (sharing stories), creative play (trip planning), and attunement play (viewing TV together, or sports, movies, theater, the Grand Canyon).[184] It has to feel like play, meaning that if there is some other more important point to it (like sex for procreation), it is not play. But some might find bringing play into the mix easier said than done, with life's demands and challenges taking up so much space. It can also be hard to add play into the mix at work, so let's take a look at that.

WORK: Play too often gets ignored at work because it is seen as the opposite of work, instead of an investment in it. According to Dr. Stuart Brown, the founder of the National Institute for Play, "When employees have the opportunity to play, they actually increase their productivity, engagement and morale. . . There is good evidence that if you allow employees to engage in something they want to do, (which) is playful, there are better outcomes in terms of productivity and motivation."[185]

So, how can we make play useful and work fun, all jumbled together so that if someone asks us whether we are working or playing, we wouldn't know and wouldn't care? There are some companies known for their culture of play. Google is one of them, where "fun activities are not just for lunch, [and] employees can get up and go play when they get tired of working on a project or answering emails."[186] So many people I know wish with all their might they could wake up in the morning wanting to go to work. Of course, if they could make it workplay, chances are they would. I mean, if they are going to do work anyway, why not?

Because playing is just not all that easy for everyone to do.

What's in the Way, and What We Can Do?

NEGATIVITY BIAS: There is something called the negativity bias that gets in the way of play in love and at work. In what we call the environment of evolutionary adaptation, millions of years ago when our modern brains were forming, if something great happened (like a mating opportunity) and we missed it, oh well, too bad, but there would be another. If, on the other hand, something terrible was coming down the pike and we missed it, we just became somebody's lunch. So it makes sense we would evolve to be more vigilant about the negative than the positive as a survival rule. We are no longer in that environment, but we live like we are, some more than others. If your partner or teammate has taken on that role of looking out for danger more than you have, it would be nice if you expressed your gratitude and took some of it on yourself. Just to be nice. And nicer still would be if you can, on purpose, plant some play into your lives, as a habit-forming staple for the long haul.

ATTENTION: It is not enough to want to do something. We have to actually be into doing it while we are doing it. And that means we have to be paying attention, exquisite attention, to what my philosophy tutors call *the working surface*. Mihaly Csikszentmihalyi calls it *flow*, the joyful state of optimal experience when we lose ourselves in what we are doing by paying single-point attention to it.[187]

We all know what it is like to be reading a book and three pages later have no idea what we just read. Or to be driving to our destination without any recall of anything on the road that took us there. On the opposite end of the spectrum lies attention to the *working surface*—where my eyes meet the words on the page when I am writing to you, where my listening receives the sound of my client's voice, or my sight receives my client's face and body language. I hope you will try this and see for yourself that joy—in love and in work—exists through the power of your attention. Guess what else is in the way of our playing in love and in work? *The look* and shame.

"THE LOOK" AND SHAME: That's right, a lot of people are reluctant to play due to fear. Fear of looking like a fool, fear of making a mistake, of being undeserving, of work undone—of rejection. You name it. Name it for yourself. For example, when the protector (a.k.a. inner critic) in you says "You have work to do," you may follow that with something like "Yes, I do, and it will be there for me when I'm done refreshing my mind to do it better." Or when the protector says, "You will look like a fool out there on that dance floor," you can agree again with something like "Yes, you are right, I might, but how I look is irrelevant for a physical activity aimed to improve how I think and feel." When the protector says, "Don't do it; you are going to get rejected," you can say, "Yeah, I might get rejected, and I won't like how that feels, but I won't die and at least I tried." And for anyone having trouble figuring out what is the best play for you, maybe find a quiet place, close your eyes, take a few beautiful belly breaths, and picture yourself as a little you on the swings, or whatever it is you loved to do as a child. Then, let how you can do that or something like that now come into view. How about, to start, designating one time a day just for play? Or something else you might devise.

VALUING PLAY: Here is a way to know when we have succeeded in making our work so satisfying that work and play are one. Ask yourself, *If I could receive the same pay, the same prospects for future pay, the same amount of approval from other people, and the same sense of doing good for the world for not doing this job as I am receiving for doing it, would I quit?*[188]

If we would do the work anyway, then we know we are in it for—and sustained in it by—the deep internal satisfaction that can fuel us to feel and do well in everything else we touch. It is a state of play, or enough like play, to reduce stress, increase motivation and productivity, boost creativity, build relationships, improve physical and mental health, and so on. How can we possibly not value that?

And that's not all. Jane McGonigal, PhD,[189] designs alternative-reality games to solve real problems for individuals and the world. Her books and other publications, and her talks and apps, extend to individuals and organizations in thirty countries and six continents around the world. Dr. McGonigal is director of Games Research & Development at the Institute for the Future, where she researches how games help us to transform ourselves and our world. Her humanitarian mission for our future is to transform the world through play, hoping that a gamer will win the Nobel Peace Prize someday.

Popular science author Steven Johnson speaks just as passionately about the importance of play in our future, in his book Wonderland: How Play Made the Modern World. He had this to say about play: "If you are trying to figure out what's coming next, you are often better off exploring the margins of play: the hobbies and curiosity pieces and subcultures of human beings devising new ways to have fun. . . . You will find the future wherever people are having the most fun."[190]

In our next and final chapter, we will talk about the

future. 'Til then, after then, and forever into the future, let us all play. Here below is a case example, and an exercise on how you can make work play.

Case Example

Deidre is a financial services professional who has an especially good working relationship with a coworker in her office, whom she considers her best friend. That's the good part. The stressful part was the unrelenting pressure to build her book of business. Deirdre had a hard time **grounding** herself in the belief that things could be different at work, unless she left—which, for a number of reasons, including her great relationship, she did not want to do. She did, however, **recognize** that her misery was unhealthy and unsustainable, that she would have to shift something somewhere, most likely inside of herself.

We did an exercise through which she could **explore** earlier times in her life when she felt happier than she had lately. What came up for her were times when she enjoyed physical activity, including but not limited to hiking with her parents. The **action** she took to get her internal and external environments into better alignment was to bring the exercise equipment she already owned out of the basement so she might actually get on it. She also planned to talk to her parents about hiking together again. Deirdre will have to **tackle** her tendency to work, work, work—harder, not smarter—as she is *Getting to Great in Work and Life*, nourishing her mind, body, spirit—and her career—through play.

Exercise:
Make. Work. Play.

A surface is the outer or topmost boundary of an object. This is the point of contact between you (or the instrument you are using) and that object. For example, where the fingers touch the keyboard, the pen touches the paper, the drill goes into the wall, the brush dips into the paint, the knife cuts the tomato, the sound of a speaker's voice hits the ear.

The normal human mind wanders about 70 percent of the time. Anchoring the attention to the point of contact between you and the surface you are working with keeps the mind from straying away from the present moment into past regrets and future worries. Work feels like play. Pleasure and performance are enhanced.

This exercise is designed to help you practice command and control of your attention, with a simple task that can be generalized across a wide variety of activities. Single-point attention brings the many benefits of play to work and life.

To Practice:

- Fill your kitchen sink with warm, sudsy water, and place your dirty dishes in it.

- One dish at a time, turn your attention to where your hand meets the liquid-detergent dispenser, where the liquid detergent meets the sponge, where the sponge meets the dish, and so on.

- Each time the mind begins to wander, and it will, gently bring the attention back to the surface of the work.

- Notice how it feels to truly engage in what one is engaged with, instead of rushing mindlessly through it all to be done rather than to live.

You never change things by fighting the existing reality. To change something,build a new model that makes the existing model obsolete.

~ Buckminster Fuller

10
FUTURE FOR US

Aimlessness

RECENTLY I WAS INTERVIEWED by a bright, young college senior whose assignment was to learn something about the life of a woman from a different generation. When she got to the part where she asked, "What were your goals for the future when you were little?" I broke out laughing. Goals? I don't remember any goals. Maybe getting out of the house was a goal, although given how good I was at getting grounded, I'm not even sure I wanted that. But that's just me. I know other women of my cohort, and certainly men, who knew all along that they would go to college and make something professional of themselves. Then again, I am the one still working for the love of it, which throws into question how much "planning for the future" is what the future is about.

As the old Yiddish saying goes, "We plan, God laughs."

Research psychologist Dan Gilbert found that most of us are pretty bad at predicting our futures altogether.[191] This inability to know the future applies not just to individuals, but to species and cultures as well.

Getting from Where to Here

Academic authors Julia Kindt and Tanya Latty give us Darwin's theory in a nutshell:

> Plants and animals produce more individuals than nature can sustain in each generation. These individuals vary in looks and in physical and behavioural characteristics, and they are able to pass on this variation to the next generation. Those individuals better suited to their environment have an advantage and are in turn more likely to survive to give their features to future generations.[192]

To repeat for emphasis: *Those individuals better suited to their environment have an advantage.* Not so simple, as environments adapt to what we are doing to them too. This is why some but not all researchers have begun to call the era we are in the Anthropocene—*Anthropos* is Greek for "human," and *cene* for Cenozoic, or the "new life" geographical time period we are in.[193] In addition to what we already know about how other species are morphing or dying because of us, consider these ideas and findings from environmental theorist Matthew Adams on what we are also doing to ourselves:[194]

- The history of Earth is 4.54 billion years old. If that history is a twenty-four-hour clock, we have been here for nineteen seconds.

- Three-quarters of all species got wiped out sixty-six million years ago, by an asteroid maybe, opening the way for dominance of mammals.

- Industrialism used up finite resources. With this, "unprecedented environmental breakdown . . . fundamentally circumscribes the long-term viability of any possible era of human dominance."

- "The history of our far future, if we have one, will be one where we learnt to recognise interdependence with nature, with other species." Either we do this or, he believes, we will cease to exist.

I find that sobering. But wait . . . he's saying that we have to recognize our interdependence with nature. Wasn't it our interdependence that built us the neural equipment that we have now? The big brain. The social brain. Aren't humans the ones equipped to imagine the past and the future, to explore alternative scenarios, and to interconnect with each other's minds to bring solutions about? We never could see exactly what the future would look like, and we still can't, but we don't have to. We are here, aren't we? So we have problem-solved in the great unknown, successfully together, before. Doesn't that mean that we can do it again?

I believe we already are. Now more than ever, we have put inequality and injustice on our collective radar screen: income inequality, race relations, environmental justice, animal rights, etc. Now we just need **grounding** in the belief that things can be better, that we are better than this. And we need to **recognize** that fitness begins with and requires that we know who we are. If we are anything, we are creatures driven—and equipped—to survive and to thrive. So let's just do that.

Getting from Here to Where

As we begin to **explore** the possibilities before us, each in our own way, let's take care that our **action** steps are not so big that they overwhelm and shut us down, but big enough that they inspire us to keep going. And let's do it in groups that are also not too big, not too little, but just right as well. Anthropologist Robin Dunbar tells us that groups not exceeding 150 in number tend to work better and longer, and more specifically that "according to the theory, the tightest circle has just five people—loved ones. That's followed by successive layers of 15 (good friends), 50 (friends), 150 (meaningful contacts), 500 (acquaintances) and 1500 (people you can recognise)."[195]

Please try hard not to get distracted by *the look* regarding how many friends you do or don't have. Getting hung up on *the look* is only one of the many old habits or tendencies to **tackle** along the way. Friends really are a case of quality over quantity, and what you think about what they think about what you think is really not the point. The point is that we choose good company—that is, others who live and breathe the values that we hold dear. Affinity groups make our aspirations feel like the norm. And because we need so much to be who we are *and* to fit in, being with others who share our deeply held values takes care of both. So, for example, for health, or spending, or environmental footprint, you can more easily overturn your own status quo by embedding with people, communities, and organizations who already have. Let's support each other. Let's build a new model together and make the old one obsolete, or grow a beautiful new garden together and let the weeds go to seed. I love these quotes:

Life is like a play: it's not the length,
but the excellence of the acting that matters.
~ *Seneca*

And

Do not be daunted by the enormity of the world's grief.
Do justly, now. Love mercy, now. Walk humbly, now.
You are not obligated to complete the work, but neither
are you free to abandon it.
~ *Rabbi Tarfon*

The times in which we live are as chaotic and uncertain as ever before. And we all have a part to play in creating the future we actually want. ***Getting to Great in Work and Life*** requires that we play our parts well—with as much joy, harmony, courage, intelligence, and compassion as we can muster for the project. We all have to take good care of who and what we count on to take care of us. This means that we take care of ourselves, each other, and the environments in which we work and live. Below you will find a case example of one woman's best effort, and an exercise to help you with your own. Please accept my sincere appreciation for your attention. I have really enjoyed this time with you and hope it will make a difference for you.

Love,
Madelaine

Case Example

Madelaine is a classically trained and licensed psychotherapist, with an MBA and board certification in executive, career, and life coaching. Through a rich series of loving relationships with people who believed in her (family, friends, teachers, therapists, colleagues, clients), Madelaine got **grounded** in the belief that she could someday find satisfaction and success in work and life. Madelaine had to **recognize** that her needs and interests were not what other people might have expected. More of an introverted egghead than most people would guess, her recognition meant coming to terms with *the look* and shame of being a little bit quirky in her quiet ways. Her long and winding **exploration** with a variety of work roles and responsibilities revealed her passion for contributing to the personal and professional growth and well-being of others. She is grateful every day of her life for the privilege and the pleasure to serve.

To create that internal–external environmental fit upon which a great life depends, the **action** she took was to leave her good job at Harvard Medical School in Boston for a move to Washington, DC. In DC, where all of her beautiful, kind, smart, loving, and funny children live, she set up shop, independently, to practice her craft. Madelaine loves her family, her friends, her clients, her work, and Raphael Leonardo, her sweet little Havanese pup. Madelaine is **tackling** a habit of making choices that recreate the *daddy drama* from her past—and she is winning. With so much love in her life, and having prevailed over life's many challenges without ever losing her smile, Madelaine feels that she is a poster child for **Getting to Great in Work and Life**, no matter what.

Exercise:
You, the Explorer

All along, life was full of new challenges and new horizons: a new teacher, a new school, new kids in the schoolyard, physical changes in our bodies and our brains. There are also the adjustments to the new that we are required to make when adult adversities enter our lives, depending on our luck and our lot. Maybe you had a moment in your life when you were the *explorer* of unknown territory without the necessary and sufficient external supports. And maybe that left you less than certain that you could cope as well as you would like with whatever comes your way now and into the future.

This exercise is designed to help you go back in time to provide yourself with a corrective emotional experience—that is to say, with an image of who and what might have been helpful then, and therefore helpful to you now.

To Practice:

• Sit comfortably in your seat, and close or just rest your eyes by gazing downward.

• Begin to feel yourself falling still, breathing in through the nose, out through the nose, belly out on the in-breath, belly in on the out-breath.

• Begin to scan your heart or mind for a time

when you might have been ready to explore some new part of your life with no one to "hold your hand."

- Can you see you then? Can you see you there? Can you imagine someone with you providing for you there, the kind of person it would be nice to have supporting you now? Might that someone even be the person you have become? Or someone else you know? To find or create real or imagined good company is an experience you give to yourself that can make more of a difference than you may know.

- *Practice, practice, practice, and see what happens . . .*

AFTERWORD AND ACKNOWLEDGMENTS

THIS BOOK WAS WAITING to happen for so many years that it appeared to be writing itself. And much like a Ouija board, there were many other fingers on the keyboard with my own. Although I heard wonderful stories about Grandmom Rose, she died years before I was born, so I never actually met her. Still, I am blessed with her wise, warm, and funny internalized voice, always there to help me find my way. I think that's what my clients mean when they say they can hear me too, even when I am not there.

I would also like to take this opportunity to come full circle with you on what it might have meant that I was *never* allowed out. A number of years ago, at a gathering with some friends who were talking about their fathers, I remembered how my father used to sit me on his knee, all wrapped up in a towel, after my bath on Sunday nights. Using the amber comb with the tiny teeth, he combed through my golden little-girl hair. At times, he would tell me stories about his father, Maurice, the Romanian tailor, barefooted in the snow, frostbitten, with a loaf of bread under his arm. He would also sing me a song called *"Daddy's Little Girl"*—"You're the end of the rainbow, my pot of gold, you're Daddy's little girl to have and to hold, a precious gem is what you are."[196]

But because he worked such long hours, he was not always there to have and to hold me. And spirited as I was, I now choose—among a variety of alternatives—to imagine that my childhood confinement was not because my father did not love me but because he did. That is, although I can never know for sure, it seems entirely plausible to me now that keeping me in the house may well have been my father's way to keep his precious little gem safe. We all get to choose what kind of story we want to live in, and this is mine. Rest in peace, my dear dad, and thank you for trying so hard and caring so much about me and how I would turn out.

My sincere appreciation as well to my co-director and dear deceased friend, Greta Rittenburg, with her undying efforts to convince me that the purpose of my misfortune was to help me "grow"; my mom, who showed me what grace under fire looked like; all the many authors sprinkled throughout this book who taught me how to make learning useful and fun; and my philosophy tutors, who taught me "the truth" about the human condition. I went to them for intellectual stimulation; they decided to heal my soul. To my mentor, Steven Nisenbaum, arguably the smartest person I have ever met, my thanks for everything you ever taught me, and for always knowing what I was talking about, sometimes better than I did myself. To Ann Ward, one could not ask for a wiser, kinder, and more intellectually and culturally helpful friend. And to my clients, every single one of you who welcomed me warmly to your journey, I cannot thank you enough for everything you taught me about the courage, commitment, and possibility of *Getting to GREAT*.

To my smart, sweet, loving, and funny children, Marlyn and Joey, and the gorgeous families they created, bless your hearts for the constant comfort—just by being who you all are—that I did a good job at the thing that mattered most, being a mom. Finally, to every other kind soul who touched my life, I thank you for your investment in me, which I hope to pay forward in full.

ENDNOTES

INTRODUCTION: WHY THIS MATTERS

1 "The US Is the Most Overworked Country in the Developed World. Here's How We'll Change That," March 1, 2018 https://www.forbes.com/sites/cartoonoftheday/2018/03/01/the-us-is-the-most-overworked-country-in-the-developed-world-heres-how-well-change-that/#57ccfd9e1880.

2 "Global Organization for Stress: Stress Solutions for the World," November 11, 2019. http://www.gostress.com/stress-levels-are-rising-worldwide/.

3 Ilja Milenkovic, "42 Worrying Workplace Stress Statistics," American Institute of Stress, September 23, 2019. https://www.stress.org/42-worrying-workplace-stress-statistics.

4 Jena McGregor, "Workplace is No. 5 leading cause of death in the U.S., professor says," *The Washington Post*, March 29, 2018.

5 John LaRosa, "U.S. Personal Coaching Industry Tops $1 Billion, and Growing," Market Research.com, February 12, 2018. https://blog.marketresearch.com/us-personal-coaching-industry-tops-1-billion-and-growing.

6 Roberto Ceniceros, "Tracking True Cost of Lost Productivity Remains a Challenge." Workforce.com, September 17, 2012. https://www.uml.edu/research/cph-new/worker/stress-at-work/financial-costs.aspx

PART I: GETTING TO GREAT AT WORK

1
WHO ARE WE? WHO ARE YOU?

7 Daniel Kahneman, *Thinking, Fast and Slow* (New York: Farrar, Straus, and Giroux, 2011), 415.

8 *Encyclopaedia Britannica,* Information Theory, https://www.britannica.com/science/information-theory/Physiology

9 Daniel Dennett, "Facing Up to the Hard Question of Consciousness," *Philosophical Transactions* (September 19, 2018), 373.

10 René Descartes, *Meditations on First Philosophy* (1641), Meditation II, 6.

11 Personal in-class communications with the School of Practical Philosophy.

12 Deepak Chopra, *Ageless Body, Timeless Mind* (NY: Harmony Books, 1993) 170.

13 Pierre Baldi, *The Shattered Self: The End of Natural Evolution* (Cambridge, MA: MIT Press 2001), 116.

14 Kevin Kelly, *Out of Control* (NY: Addison-Wesley, 1994), 55.

15 Steven Pinker, *How the Mind Works* (NY: Norton and Co, 1997), 21.

16 Steven Pinker, *The Blank Slate* (NY: Penguin Books, 2002), 32.

17 Paul Lawrence and Nitin Nohria, *Driven: How Human Nature Shapes Our Choices* (San Francisco: JosseyBass, 2002), 57.

18 Roger Fisher and Daniel Shapiro, *Beyond Reason: Using Emotions as You Negotiate.* (NY: Penguin Books, 2005).

19 Kenwyn Smith and David Berg, *Paradoxes of Group Life* (San Francisco: Jossey-Bass, 1990).

20 Scott Kaufman, "There is no nature–nurture war," *Scientific American,* January 18, 2019, https://blogs.scientificamerican.com/beautiful-minds/there-is-no-nature-nurture-war/

21 Christopher Soto, "Personality can change over a lifetime, and usually for the better, *NPR Radio,* June 30, 2005.

22 Robert Wright, *The Moral Animal: Why We Are, the Way We Are: The New Science of Evolutionary Psychology* (New York: Random House, 1994), 316.

23 Rebecca Riffkin, "In U.S., 55% of workers get sense of identity from their job," *Gallup.com*, August 22, 2014, https://news.gallup.com/poll/175400/workers-sense-identity-job.aspx

24 Derek Thompson, "Workism is making Americans miserable." *The Atlantic*, February 2019, 24.

25 Belle Beth Cooper, "Novelty and the brain: why new things make us feel so good," LifeHacker, May 21, 2013, https://lifehacker.com/novelty-and-the-brain-why-new-things-make-us-feel-so-g-508983802.

26 Wright, *The Moral Animal*, 243.

27 Clancy Martin, "Impostor syndrome: do you sometimes feel like a fraud?" *The Economist 1843*, December/January 2020.

28 Joseph Grenny, "Almost All Manager Have at Least One Career-Limiting Habit," *Harvard Business Review*, July 2016, https://hbr.org/2016/07/almost-all-managers-have-at-least-one-career-limiting-habit.

29 Kent Bailey, "Mismatch Theory," *Human Paleopsychology*, Accessed July 19, 2020, https://notes.utk.edu/Bio/greenberg.nsf/0/1bcbaf5fca6e42448525653a00068c2e?OpenDocument.

30 Anthony Gottlieb, "It ain't necessarily so: How much do evolutionary stories reveal about the mind?" *The New Yorker*, September 10, 2012.

31 Carey Fitzgerald and Kimberly Danner, "Evolution in the office: How Evolutionary Psychology Can Increase Employee Health, Happiness and Productivity," *Evolutionary Psychology*, 2012, 10(5): 770-781.

32 Wright, *The Moral Animal*, 245, 257.

33 Guy Winch, "10 surprising facts about rejection." *Psychology Today*, July 3, 2013. https://bit.ly/3cYXrrx.

34 Guy Winch, "Rejection is more powerful than you think." *Salon,* July 23, 2013. https://bit.ly/30B61u1.

35 Nicole Fisher. "Rejection and physical pain are the same to the brain." *Forbes,* December 25, 2015, https://bit.ly/2B0cbZT.

36 Winch, "10 surprising facts about rejection."

37 Ralph Waldo Emerson, *Self-Reliance and Other Essays* (Mineola, NY: Dover Publications, 1993), 19.

3

OTHER PEOPLE: HEAVEN AND HELL

38 Kirk Woodward, "The Most Famous Thing Jean-Paul Sartre Never Said," *Rick On Theater* (blog), July 9, 2010, http://rickontheater.blogspot.com/2010/07/most-famous-thing-jean-paul-sartre.html

39 https://www.goodreads.com/quotes/4262595-i-am-not-what-i-think-i-am-and-i

40 Steve Martinot, "The Sartrean Account of the Look as a Theory of Dialogue." Accessed July 19, 2010, https://www.ocf.berkeley.edu/~marto/dialogue.htm.

41 Leo Tolstoy, *War and Peace,* trans. Rosemary Edmonds (New York: Penguin, 1957), 118.

42 David Melamed, et al, "The robustness of reciprocity: Experimental evidence that each form of reciprocity is robust to the presence of other forms of reciprocity," *Science Advances,* 2020; 6 (23): eaba0504 DOI: 10.1126/sciadv.aba0504

43 Ahra Ko, "Caring for family is what motivates people worldwide," Arizona State University, December 3, 2019, https://asunow.asu.edu/20191203-caring-family-what-motivates-people-worldwide.

44 Hal Hellman, H. (2001). *Great Feuds in Medicine: Ten of the liveliest disputes ever* (New York: John Wiley and Sons, 2001), 115.

45 Wright, *The Moral Animal*, 258.

46 *Webster's New World Dictionary of the American Language* (New York: The World Publishing Company, 1960), 1033.

47 Desmond Morris, *The Naked Ape* (New York: Random House, 1967), 18. Desmond Morris said "around 15" million years, but others have said five to seven million years, e.g., P. Lawrence, and N. Nohria, *Driven* (San Francisco: Jossey-Bass, 2002).

48 University of Georgia, "Social Exclusion Changes Brain Function And Can Lead To Poor Decision-making." *ScienceDaily*. Retrieved May 30, 2008, from http://www.sciencedaily.com/releases/2006/11/061108154256.htm

49 Christine Comaford, "75% of workers are affected by bullying—here's what to do about it." *Forbes*, August 27, 2016. https://www.forbes.com/sites/christinecomaford/2016/08/27/the-enormous-toll-workplace-bullying-takes-on-your-bottom-line/#3fc55a4c5595.

50 Ase Marie Hansen, et al., "Bullying at work, health outcomes, and physiological stress response," *Journal of Psychosomatic Research*, Jan, 2006; 60(1): 63-72.

51 JL Wang, et al., "The relationship between work stress and and mental disorders in men and women: findings from a population-based study," *Journal of Epidemiology and Community Health*, Jan;62(1): 42-47.

52 Leon Sloman, "Adaptive function of depression: psychotherapeutic implications," *American Journal of Psychotherapy*. Summer 1994;48(3): 401-416.

53 Roderick Kramer, "The Great Intimidators," *Harvard Business Review*. February 2006, 88-98.

54 Ivy Broder, "Review of NSF economics proposals: Gender and Institutional patterns," *The American Economic Review*, September, 1993, 83.

55 Matt Ridley, *The Origins of Virtue* (New York: Penguin, 1996), 157.

56 Tara Madden, *Women versus Women: The Uncivil Business War* (New York: AMACOM, 1987), 34.

57 Phyllis Chessler, *Woman's Inhumanity to Woman* (New York: Nation Books, 2001).

58 Steven Pinker, *How the Mind Works*, 442.

59 Robert Sapolsky, *Why Zebras Don't Get Ulcers* (New York: Holt Paperbacks, 2005)

60 Ernest Becker, *The Denial of Death* (New York: Free Press, 1973) xvii.

61 Annette Simmons, *Territorial Games: Understanding & Ending Turf Wars at Work* (New York: AMACOM, 1997), 179.

62 Franz de Waal, "Putting the altruism back into altruism: the evolution of empathy," *Annual Review of Psychology*, 2008, 59:279-300.

63 Wright, *The Moral Animal*, 259.

64 Andrew Colman. *A Dictionary of Psychology* (Oxford England: Oxford University Press, 2009).

65 Ivette Chamorro-Florescano, et al, "Contests over reproductive resources in female," *PLOS One*, August 10, 2017. https://journals.plos.org/plosone/article?id=10.1371/journal.pone.0182931.

66 Martin Kihn, "Working with you is killing me." *Wall Street Journal*, April 4, 2006, B1.

4

MANAGING YOUR MIND

67 *Bhagavad-Gita*, trans. Ekrath Easwaran (Tomales, CA: Nilgiri Press, 2007), 259.

68 Becker, *Denial of Death*, 5.

69 Jerry Useem, "Power Causes Brain Damage." *The Atlantic.* July/August, 2017, https://bit.ly/2ZfBu2F

70 Denis Le Bihan, *Looking Inside the Brain: The Power of Neuroimaging* (New Jersey: Princeton University Press, 2014).

71 Richard Schwartz and Martha Sweeney, *Internal Family Systems Therapy* (NY: The Guilford Press; Second Edition, 2019)

72 Jon Kabat Zinn, *Wherever You Go There You Are* (New York: Hyperion, 1994), 4.

73 Antoine Lutz et al., "Regulation of the neural circuitry of emotion by compassion meditation: effects of meditative expertise." *Public Library of Science One.* March 2008, 26;3(3):e1 897.

74 Daphne Davis and Jeffrey Hayes, "What are the benefits of mindfulness," *The Monitor,* July/August 2012, Vol 43, No. 7, https://www.apa.org/monitor/2012/07-08/ce-corner.

75 Jeffrey Dusek, et al., "Genomic counter-stress changes induced by the relaxation response," *Public Library of Science One,* Jul 2008 2;3(7).

76 Benedict Carey, "Lotus Therapy," *The New York Time,* May 27, 2008. Article surveys studies of mindfulness meditation.

77 Julie Brefczynski-Lewis, et al., "Neural correlates of attentional expertise in long-term meditation practitioners," *Proceedings of the National Academy of Science,* Jul 3, 2007;104(27):11483-8.

78 Antoine Lutz, et al., Long term meditators self-induce high amplitude gamma synchrony during mental practice, *Proceedings of the National Academy of Sciences,* USA, 2004 101(46)16369-16373, 3.

79 Sara Lazar, S. et al. "Meditation experience is associated with increased cortical thickness," *NeuroReport,* (2005)16:1893-1897.

80 Paul Lehrer and Richard Gevirtz, "Heart Rate Variability Biofeedback: How and Why Does it Work?" *Frontiers in Psychology,* 2014.

81 Carryl Baldwin, et al., "Detecting and Quantifying Mind Wandering during Simulated Driving," *Frontiers in Human Neuroscience,* August 8, 2017.

82 Steve Bradt, "Working Mind Not a Happy Mind." *Harvard Gazette,* November 11, 2010. https://news.harvard.edu/gazette/story/2010/11/wandering-mind-not-a-happy-mind/

83 Gabriele Oettingen, *Rethinking Positive Thinking: Inside the New Science of Motivation* (New York: Penguin Books, 2014).

84 John Cartwright, *Evolution and Human Behavior* (Cambridge, MA: The MIT Press, 2000), 206.

5
MASTERING YOUR MOUTH

85 Francisco Aboitiz, et al., "Cortical Memory Mechanisms and Language Origins." *Brain and Language,* Jul 2006; 98(1):40-56.

86 Lise Abrams, "Tip-of-the-Tongue States Yield Language Insights." *American Scientist,* May-June, 2008, Volume 96, Number 3, 234. http://www.americanscientist.org/issues/feature/2008/3/tip-of-the-tongue-states-yield-language-insights.

87 Leonard Schlain, *The Alphabet Versus the Goddess: The Conflict Between Word and Image* (NY: Penguin Books, 1999), 14.

88 Stephen Johnson, *Mind Wide Open: Your brain and the Neuroscience of Everyday Life* (New York: Scribner, 2004), 23.

89 Anthony Stevens and John Price, *Evolutionary Psychiatry,* (UK: Routledge Press, 1996), 148.

90 Geoffrey Miller, *The Mating Mind* (New York: Random House, 2000), 354–355.

91 Cartwright, *Evolution and Human Behavior,* 208.

92 Katie Heaney, "How complaining turns co-workers into friends." *The Cut,* April 22, 2019, https://www.thecut.com/2019/04/how-complaining-turns-co-workers-into-friends.html.

93 Yudhijit Bhattacharjee, "Why We Lie: The Science Behind Our Deceptive Ways," *National Geographic,* June, 2017, https://www.nationalgeographic.com/magazine/2017/06/lying-hoax-false-fibs-science/.

94 Alex Stone, "Is Your Child Lying to You? That's Good," *New York Times,* Jan. 5, 2018, https://www.nytimes.com/2018/01/05/opinion/sunday/children-lying-intelligence.html.

95 Goodreads, https://www.goodreads.com/author/quotes/159539.Sissela_Bok

96 Neil Garrett, et al., "The brain adapts to dishonesty." *Nature Neuroscience,* Dec 2016 ;19(12): 1727-1732. doi: 10.1038/nn.4426. Epub 2016 Oct 24.

97 Katie Shonk, "What Is Negotiation?" *Program on Negotiation* (blog), Harvard Law School, April 27, 2020, https://www.pon.harvard.edu/daily/negotiation-skills-daily/what-is-negotiation.

98 Stephen Levinson, "Turn-taking in human communication." *Trends in Cognitive Sciences.* 2015, VOLUME 20, ISSUE 1, 6-14.

99 Nick Enfield, "From 'huh' to 'who'? The universal utterances that keep us talking." The Conversation. October 8, 2015, https://theconversation.com/from-huh-to-who-the-universal-utterances-that-keep-us-talking-47775.

100 Susan Nolen-Hoeksema, *Women Who Think Too Much: How to Break Free of Over-thinking and Reclaim Your Life* (New York: Henry Holt and Co., 2003), 75.

101 Ridley, *The Origins of Virtue,* 188–190.

102 Jane Elliott, "How singing unlocks the brain." BBC News. November 20, 2005, http://news.bbc.co.uk/2/hi/health/4448634.stm.

103 Jared Sandberg, "Cubicle Culture." *Wall Street Journal,* February 14, 2006, B1.

104 *Bhagavad-Gita*, 259.

PART II: GETTING TO GREAT IN LIFE

6
WORK-LIFE QUALITY

105 His Holiness Sri Shantanand Saraswati, *Good Company: An Anthology of Sayings, Stories and Answers to Questions by the Shankaracharya of Jyotir Math* (MA: Element Books, LTD, 1992).

106 Sonja Lyubomirsky, *The How of Happiness* (New York: The Penguin Press, 2007).

107 Jo Hyunju, et al, "Physiological Benefits of Viewing Nature: A Systematic Review of Indoor Experiments," *International Journal of Environmental Research and Public Health,* Dec 2019; 16(23): 4739. https://www.ncbi.nlm.nih.gov/pmc/articles/PMC6926748/.

108 Laura Spinney, "Cozy up with the Neanderthals, the first humans to make a house a home," *New Scientist,* February 9, 2019, https://www.newscientist.com/article/mg24132160-200-cosy-up-with-the-neanderthals-the-first-humans-to-make-a-house-a-home/

109 Carey Fitzgerald and Kimberly Danner, "Evolution in the Office: How Evolutionary Psychology Can Increase Employee Health, Happiness, and Productivity," *Evolutionary Psychology,* December 2012.

110 Joe Pinsker, "Are McMansions making people any happier?" *The Atlantic,* June 11, 2019, https://www.theatlantic.com/family/archive/2019/06/big-houses-american-happy/591433/.

111 Kenneth Cloke, *Mediating Dangerously* (CA: Jossey-Bass, 2001), 8.

112 Hara Estroff Marano, "Love and power," *Psychology Today,* January/February 2014.

113 Pinker, *The Blank Slate,* 442.

114 Poorna Bell, "The History of Friendship: How friendship evolved and why it's fundamental to your happiness," *Huffington Post,* February 10, 2014. https://www.huffingtonpost.co.uk/2014/02/10/history-of-friendship-evolution_n_4743572.html

115 Mayo Clinic Staff, "Friendships: Enrich your life and improve your health," April 19, 2019, https://www.mayoclinic.org/healthy-lifestyle/adult-health/in-depth/friendships/art-20044860.

116 Judah Pollack and Olivia Cabane, "Your brain has a 'delete' button—here's how to use it," *Fast Company,* May 11, 2016, https://www.fastcompany.com/3059634/your-brain-has-a-delete-button-heres-how-to-use-it.

7
BEATING THE CLOCK

117 The Coaching Tools Company, https://www.thecoachingtoolscompany.com/products/life-balance-self-care-tools-value-pack/

118 Anne Marie Helmenstein, "What Is Time? A Simple Explanation," ThoughtCo. November 26, 2019, https://www.thoughtco.com/what-is-time-4156799.

119 "Time Matters: Biological Clockworks." *Howard Hughes Medical Institute, BioInteractive.* http://www.hhmi.org/biointeractive/museum/index.html

120 J. Sandberg, "Bosses may Disagree, But a Quick Nap Shows How Smart You Are," *Wall Street Journal,* November 17, 2004, B1.

121 "Sleep Deprivation and Deficiency." *National Institutes of Health.* https://www.nhlbi.nih.gov/health-topics/sleep-deprivation-and-deficiency.

122 John Jurgensen, "When Life Begins at 5: A New Wake-up Call," *Wall Street Journal,* March, 2006, 25–26, 1.

123 Francesco Cappuccio, et al., "Gender-specific associations of short sleep duration with prevalent and incident hypertension: the Whitehall II Study," *Hypertension.* Oct 2007;50(4):693-700.

124 Johns Hopkins Medicine: https://www.hopkinsmedicine.org/health/wellness-and-prevention/oversleeping-bad-for-your-health.

125 Sapolsky, *Why Zebras Don't Get Ulcers*, 236.

126 Jason Ong, et al. (2008). "Combining mindfulness meditation with cognitive-behavior therapy for insomnia: a treatment-development study," *Behavioral Therapy*, June 2008 39(2):171-82.

127 "A Walk Through Time: The Evolution of Time, Measurement through the Ages," National Institutes of Standards and Technology. Accessed July 19, 2020, http://physics.nist.gov/GenInt/Time/time.html.

128 Ken Wilbur, *No Boundary: Eastern and Western Approaches to Personal Growth* (Boston: Shambala, 2001), 59.

129 "How much sleep do we really need?" National Sleep Foundation. Accessed July 19, 2020. http://www.sleepfoundation.org/site

130 Wilbur, *No Boundary*, 88.

131 William James, *Principles of Psychology* (New York: Holt, 1890), 403.

132 John Ratey, *A User's Guide to the Brain: Perception, Attention, and the Four Theaters of the Brain* (New York: Vintage, 2002), 114.

133 "Time Management: Beat work overload. Increase your effectiveness. Achieve much more." MindTools. http://www.mindtools.com/pages/main/newMN_HTE.htm.

134 Daniel Everett, "Cultural Constraints on Grammar and Cognition in Pirahã," *Current Anthropology*, Volume 46, Number 4, August–October, 2005.

135 Rafael Núñez and Eve Sweetser, "With the Future Behind Them: Convergent Evidence From Aymara Language and Gesture in the Crosslinguistic Comparison of Spatial Construals of Time." *Cognitive Science*, 2006, 30 (2006) 401-450.

136 Psychiatrist Jay Feierman had this to say about the Navajo and time on 5/17/2006 listserv posting, with permission of the author on 7/7/2006.

137 Eckhart Tolle, *The Power of Now* (Canada: New World Library, 1999), 46-47.

138 Deepak Chopra, *Ageless Body, Timeless Mind* (New York: Harmony Books, 1993), 32.

139 Carl Honore, *In Praise of Slowness: Challenging the Cult of Speed* (San Francisco: Harper, 2005).

140 Honore, *In Praise of Slowness.*

8

CONCERNING MONEY

141 Northwestern Mutual Foundation has a website, The MINT, http://www.themint.org/index.html, to help parents talk with their children about money.

142 Lawrence, *Driven*, 57.

143 Erik Erikson, "Identity and the Life Cycle." *Psychological Issues*, 1959, Vol.1., No.1, 68.

144 Klaus Fliessbach, et al. "Social comparison affects reward-related brain activity in the human ventral striatum." *Science*, November 23, 2007.

145 Jeanne Fleming and Leonard Schwarz, *Isn't it* Their *Turn to Pick UP the Check?* (New York: Free Press, 2008), 82–83.

146 Stevens, *Evolutionary Psychology*, 68–70.

147 English Language and Usage. https://english.stackexchange.com/questions/214999/for-he-that-fights-and-runs-away-may-live-to-fight-another-day-wisdom-or-moc

148 Darrin McMahon, *Happiness: A History* (New York: Atlantic Monthly Press, 2006), 468.

149 Glyn Davies, "Origins of Money and of Banking: What is Money?" Accessed July 19, 2020, http://projects.exeter.ac.uk/RDavies/arian/origins.html.

150 Terence Burnham, "High-testosterone men reject low ultimatum game offers," *Proceedings of the Royal Society, Biological Sciences,* September 2007 22;274(1623):2327–30.

151 Golnaz Tabibnia, "The Sunny Side of Fairness: Preference for Fairness Activates Reward Circuitry (and Disregarding Unfairness Activates Self-Control Circuitry)," *Psychological Science.* Volume 19, Issue 4 339–347, April 2008

152 "What Is Spending Addiction—And How Do I Know If I Have It?" Partners HeathCare, Accessed July 19, 2020, http://www.eap.partners.org/WorkLife/Addiction/Compulsive_Spending/What_is_Spending_Addiction.asp?nav=leftnavigation1

153 "Stress in America 2019." *American Psychological Association.* Accessed July 19, 2020, https://www.apa.org/news/press/releases/stress/2019/stress-america-2019.pdf

154 Donna Fuscaldo, "Most Americans struggling financially despite the strong economy." *Forbes,* November 15, 2019. https://www.forbes.com/sites/donnafuscaldo/2019/11/15/most-americans-struggling-financially-despite-the-strong-economy/#4fdcd14a4b6b

155 "Stress in the Time of Covid-19." American Psychological Association. Accessed July 2020, https://www.apa.org/news/press/releases/stress/2020/stress-in-america-covid.pdf.

156 Michelle Fox, "Coronavirus crisis is causing financial stress for nearly 9 in 10 Americans," CNBC, April 16, 2020.

157 R. Sapolsky, "Investigating the Mind 2005: The Science and Clinical Applications of Meditation, November 8–10," Mind and Life Institute, http://www.mindandlife.org/media.itm05.html.

158 Sapolsky, *Why Zebras Don't Get Ulcers.*

159 Danai Chanchaochai, "The pain of one arrow." *Bangkok Post*, July 5, 2005. The article says that the quote is a translation from the Samyutta Nikaya (part of the Buddhist scriptures) http://www.buddhistchannel.tv/index. php?id=6,1408,0,0,1,0.

160 https://www.goodreads.com/quotes/7753363-forces-beyond-your-control-can-take-away-everything-you-possess

161 Kabat-Zinn, *Wherever You Go*, 4.

162 Kristen Wong, "We're All Afraid to Talk About Money. Here's How to Break the Taboo," *New York Times*, August 28, 2018, Accessed July 19, 2020. https://www.nytimes.com/2018/08/28/smarter-living/how-to-talk-about-money.html.

163 Wong, "We're All Afraid to Talk About Money."

164 Olivia Millan and Karina Piskaldo, "Men, Women and Money: Money is a hidden- but loaded- issue in most relationships." *Psychology Today*, January 1, 1999, https://www.psychologytoday.com/us/articles/199901/men-women-and-money.

165 Suze Orman, *The 9 Steps to Financial Freedom: Practical and Spiritual Steps so You can Stop Worrying* (New York: Three Rivers Press, 1997), 133.

166 "Quotes by Theragatha." GAIA Community, Accessed July 19, 2020. https://www.dailyzen.com/quotes/real-peace.

9

POWER OF PLAY

167 "Characteristics of Playful Experiences," The Lego Foundation. Accessed July 19, 2020. https://www.legofoundation.com/en/why-play/characteristics-of-playful-experiences/

168 Joe Robinson, "The Missing Link to Life Satisfaction: Play." *Working Smarter* (blog), Accessed July 19, 2020.https://www.worktolive.info/blog/topic/play-and-stress.

169 Lawrence Robinson, et al. "The Benefits of Play for Adults," HelpGuide, Accessed July 19, 2020, https://www.helpguide.org/articles/mental-health/benefits-of-play-for-adults.htm.

170 Sam Wang and Sandra Aamodt, "Play, stress, and the learning brain." *Cerebrum*, Sep-Oct; 2012:12. Accessed July 19, 2020, https://www.ncbi.nlm.nih.gov/pmc/articles/PMC3574776/.

171 David Bjorklund and Anthony Pellegrini, "Child Development and evolutionary psychology," *Child Development*, 2000 71(6), 1687-1708. https://psycnet.apa.org/record/2001-16013-018.

172 Wang, "Play, stress, and the learning brain."

173 Irene Lobata Vilo, "Why do animals play," *All You Need Is Biology* (blog), September 4, 2016.

174 Michael Tomasello, "The ultra-social animal." *European Journal of Social Psychology*, Apr 2014 ; 44(3): 187–194. https://www.ncbi.nlm.nih.gov/pmc/articles/PMC4302252/

175 Mark Maslin, "Why did humans evolve such large brains? Because smarter people have more friends," The Conversation, June 19, 2017. Accessed July 19, 2020, https://theconversation.com/why-did-humans-evolve-such-large-brains-because-smarter-people-have-more-friends-77341.

176 Wang, "Play, stress, and the learning brain."

177 Ryan Dalton "Play may be a deeper part of human nature than we thought." *Scientific American,* October 8, 2019, Accessed July 19, 2020, https://www.scientificamerican.com/article/play-may-be-a-deeper-part-of-human-nature-than-we-thought/.

178 Bjorklund, "Child Development," 1691.

179 Jake Miller, "Flights of Fancy." *Harvard Medicine,* Winter/Spring 2014, 16. Accessed July 19, 2020 https://hms.harvard.edu/magazine/play/flights-fancy.

180 Robert and Michele Root-Bernstein, "The art and science of play." The Creativity Post. June 27, 2012, Accessed July 19, 2020, https://www.creativitypost.com/article/the_art_and_science_of_play.

181 "How to Role Play With Your Lover or Spouse," wikiHow, June 16, 2020, Accessed July 19, 2020, https://www.wikihow.com/Role-Play-With-Your-Lover-or-Spouse

182 René Proyer and Lisa Wagner, "Playfulness in Adults Revisited," *American Journal* vol. 7, no. 2, 2015.

183 Stuart Brown, MD, *Play: How It Shapes the Brain, Opens the Imagination, and Invigorates the Soul* (New York: Penguin, 2010,) 166.

184 Brett and Kate McKay, "30 days to a better man day 24: Play," Art of Manliness, February 20, 2020, Accessed July 19, 2020, https://www.artofmanliness.com/articles/30-days-to-a-better-man-day-24-play/.

185 McKay, "30 Days."

186 "The power of play at work." *Huffington Post.* December 6, 2017, Accessed July 19, 2020, https://www.huffpost.com/entry/the-power-of-play-at-work_b_12011462

187 Mihaly Csikszentmihalyi, *Flow: The Psychology of Optimal Experience* (New York: Harper Perennial, July 1, 2008).

188 Peter Gray, "The Value of Play I: The Definition of Play Gives Insights." *Psychology Today.* November 19, 2008.

189 Jane McGonigal's website: https://janemcgonigal.com/meet-me/

190 Steven Johnson, *Wonderland: How Play Made the Modern World* (New York: Riverhead Books, 2016), 15.

10
FUTURE FOR US

191 Daniel Gilbert, *Stumbling on Happiness* (CA: Vintage Press, March 20, 2007).

192 Julia Kindt and Tanya Latty, "Guide to the Classics: Darwin's *On the Origin of Species*," The Conversation, May 30, 2018, Accessed July 22, 2020, https://theconversation.com/guide-to-the-classics-darwins-on-the-origin-of-species-96533.

193 Julia Kindt and Tanya Latty, "Guide to the Classics."

194 Matthew Adams, "Opinion: Anthropocene doesn't exist and species of the future will not recognise it," *PhysOrg*, March 12, 2019, Accessed July 22, 2020, https://phys.org/news/2019-03-opinion-anthropocene-doesnt-species-future.html.

195 Christine Ro, "Dunbar's Number: Why we can only maintain 150 relationships," BBC.com, October 9, 2019. Accessed June 22, 2020, https://www.bbc.com/future/article/20191001-dunbars-number-why-we-can-only-maintain-150-relationships.

196 Robert Harrison Burke and Horace Gerlach in 1949. "Daddy's Little Girl," Accessed 7/22/2020, https://digitalcommons.library.umaine.edu/mmb-vp-copyright/547.

INDEX

FOMO 115, 117
formative years 96
friends, 43, 50, 55, 63, 64, 68, 88,
    94, 97, 105, 122, 123, 130,
    134, 144, 146
future 16, 23, 28, 96, 102, 107, 108,
    137, 138, 139, 142, 143, 145,
    147

G

gamma 66
genes 18, 22, 29, 50, 66, 81, 89
good company 43, 87, 88, 91, 94,
    105, 122, 144, 148
gossip 76, 77
Grandmom Rose 43, 44, 71, 88,
    101, 114, 149
G.R.E.A.T defined 8
grounding 8, 19, 22, 24, 37, 55, 68,
    82, 98, 110, 121, 124, 138,
    143, 146
groups 16, 31, 43, 46, 47, 49, 50, 75,
    76, 88, 95, 109, 115, 116, 122,
    130, 144
group size 76, 144
guidelines for goodness 34, 35

H

happiness 7, 32, 34, 35, 37, 49, 55,
    68, 69,72, 89, 91, 94, 96, 108,
    116-118, 125, 128, 138
harmony 145
Haves and Have-nots 115
healthy 7, 23, 32, 37, 38, 65, 68, 80,
    90, 91, 94, 96, 115, 118, 119,
    120, 125, 131-133, 137, 138
hedonic treadmill 118, 124
helpless 6, 44
hero 59, 60
hierarchy 46
high achieving women 26
high demand, low control job 48
higher brain 21, 47, 56, 66-70, 81
history of Earth 28, 142
Homo erectus 73
Homo habilis 73
Homo Ludens 131

Homo economicus 115
Homo sapien 29, 73
horizons 147
hot groups 47
house size 91
human hardwiring 62, 79, 129
human nature 16, 18, 19, 30, 36, 61,
    79, 91, 115, 133
human tongue 14, 71, 73
humiliation 36, 62

I

identity 18, 20, 21, 96, 123
imagination 62, 91
impostorism 25, 26
individual growth 93, 94
industrialism 143
information 14, 17, 60, 77, 88
intelligence 61, 67, 74
intentional activity 19, 89
interdependence 130, 131, 143
internal and external environmental
    27, 36, 37, 78, 132, 138
internal environment 8, 23, 27, 28,
    38, 55, 76, 78, 89, 98, 124, 128
internal-external integration 36
intimidators 48, 49, 53

J

job satisfaction 90, 112, 137
justice and equality 117, 143

K

Kabat-Zinn, Jon 65
Kahneman, Daniel 14, 58
karoshi 5
knobs and tunings 19, 20

L

language 16, 25, 73-76, 79, 80,
Lawrence, Paul and Nohria, Nitin 18
leadership 37, 61, 75, 76, 131
leader talk 75
life values 22-24, 38, 117, 124, 144

MEET THE AUTHOR

MADELAINE CLAIRE WEISS, LICSW, MBA, BCC, is a licensed psychotherapist and board-certified executive, career, and life coach. She is a former group mental health practice administrative director, a corporate chief organizational development officer, and associate director of the Anatomical Gift Program at Harvard Medical School where she spoke before the Joint Committee on the Status of Women. As a corporate trainer, Madelaine designed and delivered programs for such diverse organizations as Harvard Medical School, Legal Services Corporation, and AARP.

She has been featured on NBC, Fox TV, Bold TV, on a variety of podcasts as guest expert, including Major, Lindsey, & Africa's *Erasing the Stigma*; has written for Thrive Global, *Authority Magazine*'s Editors List, UpJourney, My Perfect Financial Advisor; and has conducted webinars for organizations, including the American Bar Association, Harvard Law School Association-MA, and MedSense via GenieCast. Madelaine is a chapter co-author in the *Handbook of Stressful Transitions Across the Lifespan*.

Contact Madelaine at www.madelaineweiss.com